THE RINCÓN NOTEBOOKS

BEFORE THE STORM

BRIAN UNGER

MISSING LINKS PRESS

THIS MANIFESTO IS DEDICATED TO

the surfing community far & wide.
May we all find perfection.
And if that's not possible,
let's have fun & live well while we're here.

AND ALSO TO:

Janice Hirschorn, 1948 – 2009,
Mikey Bellan, 1951 – 2008,
and Addison Hodges, 1959 - 2016.

She preferred animals to people.
Because they are beautiful & vulnerable.
Mikey did not care much for people, either.
Addison was some kind of bodhisattva.
He loved people.
May we find our way to perfection.

So ist also dieses Buch eigentlich nur ein Album.

Ludwig Wittgenstein

OLD
BLACK
& WHITE
NOTEBOOK

MEDIA ADVISORY

ATTENTION EDITORS: Sports Desk, News Desk, Caribbean Desk.

Rincón, Puerto Rico. January 25, 4:38 p.m. (SportsWire; Hispanic Newswire) — At 5:00 p.m. local time the *Asociación Profesional de Surfing de Puerto Rico* will announce the winners of the men's and women's divisions of the Corona Pro Rincón Surfing Competition, the final contest of Corona's 2008-2009 professional surfing competition circuit. Digital format b-roll is available for express delivery to qualified media points.

CONTACT: Lisa Incarnación, 787.823.4249. lisa@apspr.com

Old Black & White Notebook

December 27, 1992
Rincón, Puerto Rico

With Señor Wilson Aguirre flew in low over *Punta Higuero*, low enough to break cloud cover & at a few hundred feet see a dozen surfers out at Wilderness, just before the plane touched down. The water was blue-green, the whitecaps pure & salty. It was 85° & humid on the tarmac.

The plane unloaded. There were about 50 Puerto Rican families going home for Christmas, and about ten *gringo* surfers coming down for the holiday. Ramón the *publico* driver took us & our surfboards strapped to the roof of his van to Anthony & Carmen Macaluso's Puntas Surf Club. We met a friend of Anthony's on the plane, George Ruggles, a surfer from Long Island.

December 27

3 p.m. Paddled out in 7 – 8 ft. surf at *Playa Juanita* on my 7 ft. WRV fun board, a little 'under-gunned' & not really accustomed to the speed & power of this wave. I wasn't intimidated by the size *per se*, just the unfamiliarity of the wave itself – the drop, the speed, & the large crowd of 25- 30 guys constantly jockeying for position.

Back at Puntas Surf Club we had a few *Medalla* beers with Anthony's wife Carmen Macaluso. Carmen & my wife Janice talked about Anthony.

Carmen said to Janice (nicknamed E-E), "I'm going to leave him again. He says I can't surf until the season is over. He says I never work, so I can't surf. He says I have the whole summer off. It's not true. We get people from San Juan in the summer, they come out weekends." Carmen left while we were out to dinner & moved in with her sister in Aguadilla.

Later that night at the Club we had beers with George Ruggles and Dave Stiles, master wood carpenters. Ruggles rolled a huge fat joint. Stiles had won an engineering scholarship to Rutgers University, but instead opened a surfboard factory in South Jersey and became a master surfboard shaper. He now lives and shapes boards in Rincón.

I had seven drinks, which definitely did not help my surfing the next morning. I paddled out through a break called Indicators & over to Dead Man's Cove. It was small, mostly waist to chest with an occasional juicy head-high cruiser on the set. The right-handers bank up against a rock ledge where the unlucky eponymous guy named this break in an unwise decision to try a left towards the cliff, instead of a right, away from it. He paid for it with his life. Indicators wedges a little into a Sebastian Inlet-type of peak, & if you time it correctly you can get stuffed in a little barrel right after dropping in.

4:30 p.m.   E-E and I drove over to Domes Beach. She had her running shoes on & a watch. We decided to each have our respective hour of exercise, then meet at Domes & go have a few Coronas at Calypso, the beachside bar at *Playa Juanita*. Right & left-handers were cranking through Domes in consistent head-high sets and a light onshore chop. The wave faces were clean, though littered with the boogie-boarders who had temporarily taken over the break. It was a Sunday during the peak of the season. Thank god, within a few years the boogie-boarder dominance was eliminated by local short- and longboarders.

December 30

Woke up at 7 a.m. with Mark shouting down to me from his rooms on the second floor. Hadn't slept well because of lateness of dinner. Domes was at first 2-3 ft. & glassy, with only three people in the water. By 8:15 there were only 6-7 people spread out, & the sets were cranking 5-7 foot faces, large hollowish lefts and rights. Got a few decent ones. Mark got excellent lefts.

Carmen came back. We heard cartoons on the TV upstairs in their apartment, so we knew Reno was home. I heard him say, "Daddy, come here now!" I got stoned again with George.

December 31

Feliz Año Nuevo! It's New Year's Eve!

Drove into town with Mark & Haley Caravella & bought chicken, rice, tortillas, milk & bread. We barbecued chicken on the downstairs deck. E-E wanted to stay up until at least 9:30 p.m. & was making fun of me because I kept dozing off. When the Caravellas left we made out in the hallway leading to our rooms. I put E-E's back up against the stucco wall. Our lips sucked each other's mouth, necks, cheeks, chins. She slipped a hand down my trousers and felt my hard cock, smooth & unsheathed. My hand went down her ass & felt its nice medium shape. I stroked her perfect breasts. Her nipples stood out. She was wet.

Later that night she couldn't sleep because of scratchy sheets. Dirty laundry and clean clothes were scattered pell-mell thru-out the room. Chickens & roosters howled in the background. I passed out around 8:30 & didn't wake again until 5 or 6 a.m. The coffee pot wouldn't turn on. I spilled coffee & water & grounds all over the counter. E-E said, "Somehow, by the end of the day, it will be my fault that the coffee messed up."

Sunday January 3, 1993

Dinner at Red's Pizza up the hill. Me tired. Janice in a quiet mood. We played pool with Mark, Haley, and Tom Duffy. Claude Codgen came in and we played a game with him. Claude and Duffy against me and Haley. We knew a lot of the same guys from Jersey and Cocoa Beach. Claude was a legend already, first east coaster to win the Pipe Masters.

Monday January 4

E-E so tan now her teeth & the whites of her eyes shine out from her face. Her hair is black ringlets of curls spiked with fine silvery strands. She has nut-brown chocolatey skin, smooth & fine. It gives her body a youngish cast.
Men like it (& women too).
Her black eyebrows arch up from the inside corners where the eye socket meets the nose at the lower forehead. From there each side of the brow heads northwest or northeast ½ way across the eye socket where it juts suddenly straight up toward her hairline, giving her face a skeptical, inquiring demeanor. Her nose is long and aquiline, with a slight Hebraic hook, befitting her Ashkenazi heritage.

The mouth is sensuous, and the lips run long to the corners of the mouth; extremely attractive. Janice has the subtle, refined look of the Jewish intelligentsia & *haute bourgeoisie*. But she is not of those categories. She is proud working class Jewish Democrat-Socialist out of Weequahic, Newark, New Jersey; along with the Ginsbergs, Kochs, Roths, Lewis's, Williams, and other legions of interesting Ashkenazi Jews.

E-E's Proverbs

We have to give something back because we take so much.
The children have no clue from the current culture.
A foul materialism drives the social world,
forcefully, almost invisibly, "a ghost in the machine,"
so few see it, so few cognize it for what it is, so few understand the struggle.
You can take & take & take. But then the emptiness envelopes you.
And when the millions & billions of empty vessels stare you in the eye,
you understand and begin to think, "Maybe there is something I can give."

E is my teacher, a natural bodhisattva.
She didn't have a lot of training in the monastery, but she got enough,
how subtle her teaching!

Wednesday January 6

5:30 p.m.   E just got out of the shower. We returned from *Playa Jobos* &
opened green bottles of Heineken. Surfed "Middles" at 2-4 feet with a light-medium
crosswind. Waves had power snapping on the rock reef. I was lightly bruised
on the inside coral.

   At *Jobos* we met a guy from Huntington Beach who just moved here. Nice
guy, was wearing a "Rockin' Fig" sweatshirt. He knows Fig, Parmenter, & Chris
Hawk. I'm thinking of getting a 7'8" long, 20" wide Hawk gun for larger waves.
Had chicken and fried plaintains at Señor González' bar on the beach.

6:45 p.m.   E has coined a new term for a whole category of concern: **S.W.O.G.**,
Sex With Other Girls. She said it's the only thing personal & private she will ever
ask me about in an inquisitive manner: **S.W.O.G.**

January 9

   Back in N.J.
   The flight into Kennedy:

   (1) the dipping wing scare
   (2) the cute steward
   (3) the drive home (uneventful) – (Chuck Kunes got us at JFK)
   (4) it's cold, dark & gray at home;
        we are not pleased upon our arrival.

        We are not pleased.

JANICE'S BROWN BUDDHA JOURNAL

Janice's Brown Buddha Journal , 2002

What is Buddhism?
Drink the tea and go!
Detached ? Never easy for me.
Be detached, 60s style !
If you want monogamy marry a swan.
Reason for male infidelity: men are seed scatterers.
Need to scatter seed in as many places as possible.
IT'S GENETIC!

American troops expressed disappointment when told
there would be no U.S. intervention. Someone was
quoted as saying, "they were pumped and ready to go
& they're disappointed."
No bang-bang shoot 'em up today boys!
Friendly fire – that's what we call killing our own boys.

The mating call: flirtatious to friendly and back again.
Homosexuality –
Men: genetic mainly.
Women: conscious choice mostly.

January 25

Just try not to be unhappy –
watching the birds, the sky, the cold wind –
that's using time wisely

February 7

B thinks he seduced me away from Greg, first husband
but that's his ego talking. Fact is, I was ready to leave Greg
after 15 years, when B fell in love with me.
B said he had to have me.
That's how men talk. So stupid, but we had fun.
He took me places. We went to New York,
to Hogan's Pub, with the Irish drinkers who write books.
We went to Fanelli's to eat
driving home in the snow,

At Hogan's Cork was one of the rudest assholes I ever met,
so rude and mean to me, for no particular reason,
and B's best friend.

rule #1: no more writers
rule #2: no more Irish

March 20,
Retreat with Norman Fischer,
Samish Island, Washington

We are doing a Zen *sesshin* – a weeklong retreat.
It is the fourth day of about six.
Very difficult, very painful now.
It's fucking impossible to be in the present moment,
so why doesn't he stop talking about it?
Norman says the self is nothing but an accumulation of habits.
Yes, it's true, as the buddhists say,
there's no separate autonomous thing called a self or a soul;
we are really just a 'stream' of interconnected elements,
and the stream includes both mental and physical factors.
Wow, I am a stream. I always felt like a stream.

Of course there is something which holds the stream together,
but that doesn't make it permanent.

Each of us is just one little temporary stream, not eternal,
not permanent; a wavelet in the vast ocean of being.
Eventually we smash up on the far shore & disappear
in the sands of time.

I told Norman I can't understand my motivation
for certain behaviors & reactions.
Try, he said, please try to be in the present. Life is too painful otherwise.
Give yourself a break, Janice!
Just sit. Just be. Just just just.

As for B, he'll tell me what he can; and it won't be everything –
the rest will be reserved for the boys at Hogan's, and his fantasies.
I get it.

Now there's a foundation for building trust.
The building blocks of trust are his decisions,
his karma. I will decide for myself.

For Brendan happiness is doing whatever he wants without anyone
getting angry, or him getting caught...
At 36 that's called being single.

"E," he said to me this morning, "what's it like being you?"
No different from being anybody else, I suppose.

March 21, Retreat with Norman, cont'd

It's going to be this *sesshin* or bust for me. Instant enlightenment.
Just add water and mix.
Delusions.
There have been at least a half-dozen to a dozen this morning –
is it possible?
Does it matter?

YELLOW NOTEBOOK

&

OLD BLUE NOTEBOOK

Yellow Notebook
& Old Blue Notebook, winter '07

Rincón, January 2 - 29

To the airport with E-E and the kids so they can go back to school, and E can go back to work teaching second graders in Asbury Park. We drove up the hill to get gas and pick-up Gino, who wanted a ride to the airport. The sun was so bright we could hardly see. No *barrachos* were out yet in front of the bakery. When we got to Gino's his truck was gone and no one was home, so we figured he must have driven himself to Aguadilla. The ocean rumbled a deep low roar a half-mile down the hill. We saw big beautiful blue lines of surf rolling into the distant point at Wilderness, with long crisp lines of whitewater and spray, indicating it was double or triple overhead. We passed the old cock-fight arena where my son Carter and I watched two roosters slice each other up with razor blades taped to their claws.

I pulled up in front of the airport terminal at Aguadilla and hugged and kissed my kids, Carter, Forrest, and Emily. They had a good break playing in tide pools, studying reef life, and practicing surfing. E-E looked into my eyes. I gazed at the tiny dots, dashes, & freckles of her face, spots of time, a face edged by wisdom & experience. I thought of her as a Queen.
She said simply, "Be good Beavis, and call me tonight. I love you B," and then walked off into the terminal.

I drove back to Rincón and parked at the *colmado* at the top of the hill so I could watch their plane take off. A local *barracho* sat out front reading a newspaper. He looked up at me and nodded. I bought sweet bananas from the farmer who sells fruit and vegetables out of the baskets lined up by the entrance.

A dead dog with *rigor mortis* lay on its back across the street, four stiff legs pointing straight up in the air. Carmen drove past and waved.

Suddenly a big jet broke out of the fog & clouds and set a track up to the clear sky above. I pictured E-E with the kids seated all around her, and Gino stopping by to greet them with his usual boisterous cheer.

*

Tomorrow I will go up the hill & see Richie Fitzgerald. I am thinking of getting a painting from him, a new work that embeds a Derridean *différance*, like the one he did of Dogman, the old man who lived on the beach with his dogs. I am talking about the *différance* between colonialist/tourist perceptions of Puerto Rico, and the island's true cultural & political history; the people, the geography, the modes of colonial historiography, etc. One can see *différance* in Richie's Dogman painting. But what is perceived by the North Americans who have observed this painting over the years? Do they think it's humorous? Do they think it's ridiculous that an old man would live with a family of dogs in a palm thatch hut on a remote stretch of beach? That is what I ask you to carefully consider.

*

Richie Fitzgerald, an artist and a natural born rebel, had lived in Rincón twenty or so years before I arrived; digging in the sand, fishing, drinking, surfing, making paintings. Maybe I could persuade him to do a painting of Gomez's friend Pedro, who jumped off the Goat House roof in a fit of despair, impaling himself on a sharply cut branch below. What time of evening he jumped, no one could say, but his screams were heard across the valley. Some say he was drunk, but he told Gomez that he was in love with a woman who rejected him, and he decided to commit suicide to prove his unrequited love. The *machateros* had been out the day before clearing brush and trimming trees below the Goat House. So when Pedro fell, or jumped (several versions were bantered about), he landed on a freshly cut & sharply pointed branch that came through his asshole and up under his scrotum, cutting to the base of the penis and further up, almost completely severing and shattering the shaft. The sharp end of the pointy stick stuck out of his crotch like a second cock. Pedro screamed and howled and the entire *barrio* heard him. Casey woke up Milena on the next hill over. She told me she heard Pedro screaming, "Somebody's dying up here! Somebody's dying up here!" Rosita, the old lady in the blue house at the bottom of the hill, ran up to the Goat House, saw Pedro marooned in his misery, and ran back home to call the authorities.

The police and medical personnel arrived a long time later with four police cars, a fire engine, and two or three ambulances. They shot him up good with morphine. But for the next two and a half hours no one knew what to do while waiting for the helicopter from San Juan. Then Pedro started shouting, "Cut this thing off me! Cut this thing off me!" Finally one of the *bomberos* took charge and cut Pedro off the tree with big garden cutters and stanched the bleeding with multiple swaths of cloth. The medevac helicopter from San Juan arrived and he was loaded on a stretcher, the sharp branch still impaled through his crotch.

The following evening I went to the bar at Puntas Surf Club to have a beer with Anthony Macaluso and George Ruggles in anticipation of getting a ride to the airport to pick-up my friend Cork, who was coming down on the midnight flight from New York. We were discussing the new swell approaching Rincón when Grog Mesanko walked in looking like a Hollywood producer. On his arm was a young blonde woman from Maine named Crystal, who was very beautiful, and 26 years old. Crystal was a sharp judge of character and fun to talk to. She loved dogs and said she wanted to adopt a stray pup and take it back to Maine with her. A tribe of neighborhood dogs had set up camp just outside the Club in the woods off the road and Milena was feeding them from a big plastic food box a few times a week. She and Casey adopted a pregnant female to live in the garden in their back yard so Milena could help with the birth. Anthony was not pleased about it. He had a restaurant and a tourist hotel to run, and there were issues of cleanliness, sanitation, and order. Two of the dogs snuck into the Club the week before and chewed up the leather on the dining room chairs.

Crystal and Grog had met in the airport bar the night before, had several drinks, and then shared a ride to Rincón in Ramón Tirado's taxi. She confided in Grog that she and her boyfriend owned a sex shop back home, and she was tired of arguing with him, and especially tired of his constant criticism. She needed a break from him and from Maine's long winter. Later Grog concluded, based on some undisclosed physical evidence, that Crystal was a porn star, and her boyfriend was the porn site's webmaster.

Meantime, at the other end of the bar, Uris Seinfels was sipping Heinekens with the *Flamboyan* restaurant bartender Lorenza Arizaga, and the *San Juan Star* columnist, book reviewer, and celebrated raconteur Phil Painter. Uris is tall and gangly, with long blonde hair and big eyes. The local Puerto Ricans have nicknamed him "Daytime" because, they say, his hair is like the sun, and his eyes are as blue as the sky. Even though Painter had promised to drive me to the airport to get Cork, he was pissed because of an argument he witnessed between me and my friend and next door neighbor Papi Soto, who also worked at *El Flamboyan*. Papi was in the habit of inviting teenagers to his house to smoke pot, and they had blocked my driveway with their cars and pick-up trucks for several hours while they walked down the beach to Yico's for beer and billiards. Maybe I just over-reacted. I could have just hung out with Papi for a while. Maybe it was just that the kids were stoned and really stupid. You don't block people's driveways. It's annoying. So I yelled at Papi, who took it well, a true stoner. We were good friends.

But Painter heard I chewed out Papi Soto and it pissed him off. Finally the stupid kids came back from Yico's and moved their cars, and I apologized to Papi and the kids for losing my temper, and brought over a six-pack of *Cerveza Medalla* for them as a token of my remorse. Papi and I were very good friends, so this incident was nothing to us. However, it did piss Painter off. Uris remonstrated on my behalf, testifying to my good moral character and general standing in the community, so Painter relented and drove me to the airport in his big fat Plymouth Fury III, berating me the whole way as the Fury rolled and swayed like a boat in the roadway.

BLACK & WHITE NOTEBOOK 2

Black & White Notebook 2

June 5, 2009

Zoketsu Norman Fischer took the red eye from San Francisco to Newark the day Janice died in our bedroom, in our house by the ocean in Jersey. It was June, lush green outside the sliding doors to our garden full of songbirds, flowers, and vegetables; our cats' jungle lair. June is a good month in Jersey, along with May, after the long bitterness of winter. Ocean water temperatures begin to rise. Surfing is not so painful.

As Janice lay dying our cats Peter Potter, Luke, and Lea lay strewn all over our bed cuddling with her, while our dog Coquito tried to shunt them away. They were as much a part of our lives as our children, nieces, nephews, cousins, and in-laws; one family, part human, all mammalian. Peter Potter was also known as Spot, or Spotty. He had big black circle spots on a pure white coat of fur, like a moo-cow, and he moved slowly and deliberately around the house like an old man, unless he was running away from Lea, who tortured him mercilessly in her bid for alpha-female status in the cat universe.

Pete's daily exercise was to plod around the outside rim of the house in a circle, over and over again, sluggishly, three, four, or five times, and then report back inside after basking in the sun for a half-hour. Six or seven years earlier a veterinarian had diagnosed a serious heart ailment in Pete, giving him 6 months to live. But he lived another six or seven years, self-managing his cardiology with bed rest and an exceedingly lethargic lifestyle.

Luke, Petey Spot's half-brother, was an extraordinarily pleasant and extro-verted long-haired gray tabby, of medium length, with an expressive face.

He loved people, and he really loved Spot. They were best friends. However, after two or three years of male bonding and familial bliss, I brought Lea to the house from Puerto Rico and it was a big mistake. While lovely to her human parents, Lea was a bitchy, bossy redhead to her new cat step-brothers. Petey Spot was not a fighter, and Lea enjoyed nothing more than staging a sneak attack on him to strike fear & loathing into his defensive posture.

Beside the cats and the various birds that Janice fed and cared for, Coquito was Janice's clear favorite, by far the smartest mammalian animal that any of us had ever lived with, a Sheltie Mix pup. I found her on the ridge overlooking *Playa Juanita* in Rincón when she was one or two weeks old. Over time she learned

fifty or more words in English, including all of our kids' names, plus "beach," "walk," "outside," "snack," "good girl," "I love you," etc.

During Janice's last few weeks Petey's health also went into a tailspin. His heart was failing. He started behaving strangely, and then he disappeared for a week, as cats do when they feel death coming on. We were worried that he crawled off into the nearby woods and we would never see him again, but he came back and crawled into bed with her yesterday. They lay in bed together gazing into each other's eyes. I overheard Janice cooing, "Oh Petey Potty Boy, it's okay Petey, don't worry. We're going to be okay, Petey Boy, I promise you. Just cuddle here with me." They comforted each other, and kissed, and stared into each other's eyes. It was a moment, a spot of time.

In her final few days Janice lay in bed in an impenetrable semi-conscious state, her chest heaving, her breathing heavy and labored, indicating the proximity of her final transition. She was neither conscious nor unconscious; in what the Tibetan Buddhists call the *bardo* stage, in-between life and death, neither here nor there. Her face reacted when we said her name, but she could not see, could not speak, and could not wake up out of this state. I wanted to talk to her, and really wished the doctors could wake her up, even for just a few minutes or a half-hour so we could have our final words and I could tell her again how much I loved her. We were shocked, standing around in the kitchen. It was me, her sister Linda and husband Kenny, her first husband Greg, Greg's sister Leslie, my children Forrest, Emily, and Carter, her niece Jenn, my sister Christine, and the bizarre nurse from the back woods of South Jersey.

Janice was well prepared for death; no fear, no questions, and while it might seem strange for a Jew, in her final months Janice enjoyed watching 'born again' Christian preacher Joel Osteen on TV, not so much for his theology, but for his faith, his positivism, his infectious belief that life is good, that we are all going to be okay, and that we are spiritual beings in a spiritual universe.

*

On the last day before she passed into eternity, the nurse, who seemed to know nothing about how to deal with a dying person's family, told us that while Janice's external sense organs were shutting down one by one, the faculty of hearing was frequently the last to go. So, she said, be mindful of what you say while you are in the same room as Janice. It turned out to be the most intelligent and perceptive thing she said all month.

Driven by her love for Janice, Linda, who Janice loved even more than me, went into the bedroom and laid down alongside her sister and whispered in her ear that she loved her, that she would miss her, that it was okay to "go" when she wanted to, and that we all, every one of us, loved her very much.

Tears rolled out of Janice's eyes. She could hear. Her being-in-the-world was nearly invisible to us in the shell of *bardo*, but she was still alive inside, with consciousness. I came into the bedroom, saw Janice crying, and I was stunned. I lay down beside her and whispered in her ear that I loved her and would cherish her forever.

We pass through stages on the way to nirvana. You can recognize them if you pay attention and practice dutifully, whatever your practice is; but modern medicine & pharmaceutica are corrupt with money & power. It is a mistake to believe in them like religion.

The ancient buddhists and yogis in Tibet and India studied life & death for thousands of years. They paid close attention to detail and wrote down the components and sources of consciousness, the human body & biology, the cosmos, and the various stages of life & death. They created complex discourses. They were the first scientists, way before Aristotle & the other Greeks. In fact, the Greeks very likely got their initial scientific inspiration from India.

*

A day or two later Janice's family was in the kitchen with Forrest, Emily, Carter, my sister Christine, the nurse from South Jersey, our friend Bobbi Elias,

the artist Robyn Ellenbogen, and Allen Ginsberg's cousin Mindy Gorlin. I wanted
to be close to Janice because her breath was increasingly labored, so I left them
at the kitchen counter and went to her bedside, arriving just in time to see Janice
draw her last breath, slip into peacefulness, and exit the triple world; this 'container' world delimited by the five sense faculties (the *indriyas*), the sixth faculty
of consciousness, the major biophysical formations, and the socio-tribal psychology of human beings. These 'factors' and formations come together to construct
each person's narratological idea of the self – how we think and write and tell
people who we are; the stream that is us, the bundle of things that formulates
the idea of the self.

B & W
NOTEBOOK 3

...human beings are not born once and for all on the day their mothers give birth to them, but that life obliges them to give birth to themselves.

Gabriel García Márquez

B & W Notebook 3

15 January 2012
Sunday

Garrulous Plump Cork O'Reilly is flying down here from New York tonight. What an asshole; a dear friend to be sure, but what an asshole. Cork has no shame; bragging incessantly about his novels, his female conquests, and his masterful knowledge of football and baseball. But I always get the feeling that inside his fat belly is the gnawing emptiness of not being good enough; of being small in the big city, of being working class in a town defined by rich people, famous writers, fake writers, famous actors, fake actors, producers, fake producers, etc., etc., *ad infinitum*.

Fuck it. I am going to tell the truth about Cork, at least until the moment I forgive him. His desperation to be a famous writer reeks. He wants to sit at the end of the bar at Hogan's Pub as the writer the bartender fawns over, the Hemingway, Behan, Eileen Myles, or Richard Price; the one people listen to in awe while he or she gets drunker and drunker spewing bitter pearls of wisdom. Cork thinks fame is owed to him as a writer because he is a native of both Dublin and Greenwich Village, as if that really fucking matters. He thought that with this supposedly perfect birthright he would drink and write, and stroll into fame and fortune, especially fame. It could have happened, but he wasn't a good listener, he didn't study properly, and there was nothing between his ears but booze and cocaine. In my view, he didn't really listen to or study his buddies David Markson and Joel Oppenheimer, nor Eileen Myles. It was too far a reach for Cork, and that was too bad. He could have learned a lot from them.

After LaSalle Academy in the East Village, Cork read English, Irish, and American Literature at Marist College in Poughkeepsie, and then did graduate studies at Hunter College, CUNY, where he dropped out after a semester or two listening to Ivy League-trained professors prattle on about French theory and Harold Bloom (it was the height of the Bloom years in literary criticism). His true muse resided at Hogan's, off Sheridan Square in the Village, and he did eventually produce a trio of quite acceptable, fairly well written novels. The only problem was he packed his stories with worn out Roman Catholic mythology, and that *mythos* was already way dead for any serious New Yorker. He should have at least gotten an update from the Jesuits over at St. Peter's College in Jersey City, or Fordham University up in the Bronx.

Cork and I are the best of friends, I should admit that, but we are very different people. I am sorry about going off on him, and I will move on from this anger I am feeling towards him. But first I have a bone to pick with him, so that he understands something about me and my late wife, Janice.

She was a very strong & wise individual, and Cork mocked and tortured her mercilessly and rudely. There was something about her simple, deep wisdom and selfless authenticity that nagged him. His idiotic ignorance had to reign supreme in every conversation, so much so that she eventually refused to go to Hogan's with me. I often wondered how he could regurgitate this Roman Catholic mythology and hagiography *ad nauseam* while a real saint, Janice, was sitting right in front of him flesh and blood.

Cork's real literary heroes were Hogan's Pub writers like Joe Flaherty, Pete Hamill, Frank McCourt, and Jimmy Breslin, whereas I loved the scholarship of literature and the literature of scholarship. Frankly, I was stuck in the sickly trance of post-modernism sold by the mainstream Ivy Leaguers. I didn't see the way out that was being trail-blazed by poets like Frank O'Hara, Alice Notley, and Ted Berrigan. I was oblivious of them, plus Charles Olson, Diane di Prima, David Henderson, Joel Oppenheimer, Amiri Baraka, Jack Kerouac, Anne Waldman, and

Allen Ginsberg. These were people who traipsed in and out of Hogan's and other local pubs and cafés, and I should have and could have cultivated them, studied with them, drank beer and whiskey with them. They were accessible, and they had blasted very solid aesthetic paths past Pound, Stein, Eliot, and the dominant neo-modernism.

Tuesday 17 January

Cork flew in two nights ago with Rory Callaghan, the gay activist. Ramón picked them up at the airport with a cooler of Heinekens. I gave them the downstairs 'guest quarters' on the first floor; two large bedrooms, a combo living & dining room, a kitchenette, and a deck facing the aquamarine Caribbean Sea. Cork's girlfriend Mary North usually spends the night here when Cork is in town, even though she has a house a few miles up the hills of *Barrio Cruces*. Last night we hung out on the second floor deck talking, drinking *mojitos*, smoking pot. Unfortunately I promised Cork that we would make coffee first thing in the morning and go over a poem he had written. Poetry's a new thing for him. He never wrote a poem before, and it's a highly complex field now. He wants my help getting published because I edit a literary magazine called *Zen Monster*, which is more or less a product of the West Coast Zen tradition of Mike McClure, Diane di Prima, Philip Whalen, Gary Snyder, Amy Evans McClure, Joanne Kyger, Jane Hirschfield, Norman Fischer, Denise Newman, et al., with the New York schools, Language poetry (especially buddhist Language poetry), and St. Mark's Poetry Project poets thrown in.

Moreover, not only am I not the poetry editor, I don't know that much about poetry, good or bad. I know what I like, but I don't really know much else. I am not at all influential in the poetry world, and yet Cork seems to think I can turn him into the American Seamus Heaney. I never should have promised to go over

this poem he wrote. I should have pushed him over to Denise Newman and Hank Lazer, the poetry editors of *Zen Monster*. They know what they're doing. They've been doing it for decades.

When I woke up this morning I just wanted to sit *zazen* quietly with a cup of French Roast coffee from McNulty's in the West Village, and then work on one of my own writing projects, hoping Cork would sleep in and forget about our appointment to go over his poem.

I sat on my meditation cushion slipping in and out of the folds and innards of consciousness, thinking but not thinking with any structure or fixed narrative.

You can't really call it thinking in Zen meditation, because it's more like semi-conscious dreaming and drifting about peacefully. Yet sometimes an interior discourse emerges, and this morning it did. I sat there telling myself inside my head that I am not really Puerto Rican, though I live here, pay taxes here, vote here, etc. I am for Puerto Rican independence, but I am a colonial son of the North American invaders that conquered this island and have owned it for over a hundred years. Then I started thinking, why not see myself as an immigrant nationalist like the Italian, French, Corsican, Majorcan, and other Mediterranean immigrants who came here in the 19th century to farm coffee and sugar. They eventually blended in (or tried to blend in) with the native *campesinos*, although as white people they were immediately given farms and slaves by the Spanish Crown, and were thereby immediately inducted into the upper-middle classes. Still, many of them eventually became nationalists and patriots, so I could too.

Tourism is the modern expression of colonialism, right? American tourists come to Rincón and they don't know a fucking thing. They don't know how we got here, how they got here – they are almost to a person blissfully ignorant of the simplest facts of Caribbean history, Puerto Rican history, and the U.S. occupation. It's embarrassing, but I don't think I've ever met a single American who's read anything decently intelligent about the history of Puerto Rican-U.S. relations. Then they come here for a few days and act like they own the place.

As I sat there meditating ocean swells heaved and whispered on the reef beyond my back yard fence, and I realized that truthfully, Puerto Rico is a nation, a pure nation, the planet's oldest colony, and no matter how you spin it, colonialism is political and economic slavery. Dumb people fear history; fear it, forget it, and then let the propaganda idiots re-write it.

While I was telling myself this inside my head Cork came up the outdoor steps to my rooms on the second floor with an empty coffee mug in one hand and a sheaf of yellow lined paper in the other (his poem, hand-written). He told me the night before that it was a buddhist poem inspired by Jack Kerouac, and it was the first poem he had ever tried to write. Poetry requires years, decades of serious study and practice, not a couple of weeks, at least I knew that much. I should have immediately delivered him straight to Denise and Hank.

I could feel Cork peering in at me through the screen door, his belly drooping over low-hanging beltless shorts. He did a mock Asian bow and proclaimed "O Zen Buddha my teacher!" jarring me out of my trance. Then he began chanting the Heart Sutra in a silly voice. It's the ancient Mahayana Buddhist scripture that goes like this:

> "Avalokitesvara Bodhisattva when practicing deeply the *Prajna Paramita* sutra perceived that all five *skandhas* in their own being are empty, and was saved from all suffering, O Śhariputra, form does not differ from emptiness, emptiness does not differ from form, that which is form is emptiness, that which is emptiness form— the same is true of feelings, perceptions, consciousness, impulses – "

"Hey man, I came up to read you my Kerouac poem," Cork opened the screen door and came in. "We were going to have coffee, remember? This is important, Dude. Kerouac came into Hogan's a few times with David Markson."

"No – I mean, yeah," I said, back-pedaling. "I'm sorry man, I need to write a paper on Olson and Whalen this week, so I'm really busy. If you and Mary and her little friends could just leave me alone until nine-thirty, or even ten o'clock in the morning, that would be great. My deadline is Monday. Can we do this Kerouac thing later?" Cork felt that I was blowing him off on a project that was deeply important to him, which I was.

"You're bumming me out, Laddy. We were supposed to spend an hour or two this morning... and why do you bring up Mary and her friends? I can't believe it bums you out that they come over in the morning. What the fuck, Brendan, you have a stick shoved up your ass?"

"Cork, I'm not bumming out, it's totally cool, just ask them to talk quietly when they're in the back yard in the morning. Their voices carry up here when I'm writing and their inane conversations fill my head – I can't think, I can't write, and I've got to submit this paper on Monday."

"Inane?" Cork's insides quivered. "Did you really fucking say *inane*?"

"Yeah, no, you know Corky... not inane in a negative sense – just – like, I mean, *difficult for me*..."

"This is getting negative, Bro," Cork cut in. "I come upstairs to read you my poem, which we *both* decided to do, and all I get is bad vibes in paradise," he said, shaking and waving the yellow sheets of hand-written poetry in one hand and his empty coffee mug in the other.

"Sorry Dude," I tried to assuage Cork. "I want to check out your poem. I'm psyched about it, and I'm going to send it to the poetry editors at *Zen Monster*. You know I dig Kerouac, especially that book *Some of the Dharma*. We'll do it tonight, invite Rory and Mary and her friends over. We'll watch the sunset. I'll make *mojitos*."

But the anger in Cork's belly consumed any shred of amiability he had left, and he ripped up the poem into a dozen pieces of paper. They floated down the column of air like little yellow birds.

"Dude, what are you doing? Did you make a copy?"

"Fuck you! It's too fucking depressing to be around you, Brendan," Cork declared, and turned and went back down the steps to the first floor with his empty coffee mug. I stared at the rectangle of doorway and the sparkling blue patch of ocean beyond.

"I'm sorry, man," I shouted.

Cork hustled down past the steel-mesh animal cages that littered the underside of the house next door. His girlfriend Mary, an E.R. doc at the local medical center, was doing yoga in the living room. Rory was sound asleep in the bedroom off the kitchen. Cork opened a cabinet in the kitchenette, took out a bundle of coffee filters, and stuffed one into the plastic basket of a miniature Mr. Coffee machine. A brown speckled *lagartija* was perched on a metal hurricane slat in the kitchen window gazing at the bright orange guts of a papaya sprawled across the counter, its juices spilling everywhere. Cork shoved his left hand into the bag of corn chips lying in the pool of papaya juice and crammed a handful into his mouth. With his right hand he scooped several spoons of *Café Rico* into the crinkle-edged coffee filter, his face steaming red. He blurted out "sonuva-fuckin' bitch" and the gecko leapt off the hurricane slat and scurried out of sight. Rory didn't hear the expletive, but Mary did, stretching out her long tan legs and pushing her perky buns barely covered by white bikini bottoms up toward the ceiling.

"Honey, are you okay? I thought you were going to recite your poem to Brendan?" Mary piped in from the living room. She extended her legs out in a 180-degree arc, with arms and fingertips pointing out to each side in a straight line across her torso, while Cork seethed in the kitchenette. Meanwhile a few thousand Puerto Rican ants marched in martial formation towards the puddles of papaya juice and the open honey jar sitting alongside Mr. Coffee. The gecko was back on the window slat observing the entire delicious scene. Cork reached under the sink, grabbed a container of blue liquid chemicals and sprayed the ant army, extinguishing their little lives forever. The *lagartija* blanched in shock at this inhumane attack on wildlife and darted through a crack in the window frame as the metallic blue chemicals drenched the counter where human food was prepared. Cork wiped it off with a paper towel.

"He didn't want to hear the poem," he shouted in to Mary, who was now focused on her yogic breathing. "He was busy meditating, and when Brendan practices Zen other people aren't included. It's private, selfish, the opposite of real buddhism."

"Wow, that doesn't sound good," Mary retorted from a backbend pose, palms flat on the floor. "Honey, isn't it in Dōgen – or maybe it's the Fox Kōan – where it says everyone is equal, subject to the same karma, no private enlightenment.[1]

---

[1] Eihei Dōgen Zenji (1250-1253). Zen Buddhist monk, priest, teacher, founder of the Sōtō school of Zen. The term kōan is explained at footnote 21, pg. 160.

Nothing special, right?"

Watching Mr. Coffee spurt his watery brew, Cork thought of the thick, dark French Roast from McNulty's in the West Village that Brendan promised to make for them.

"Let's face it, Mare, college professors are mostly assholes, anyway," Cork replied.

"Yeah, ever since Janice died he's been weird, depressed," Mary added. Cork came into the white-washed living room with his mug of see-through coffee. Mary was stretched over the couch now, her palms firmly planted on one arm rest, her knees eight or ten inches apart in the center of the couch, with her buns pointing up. Cork fixated on the milky curve of her ass and came to stand alongside her white bikini bottoms. His cock hardened, and he slipped his hand under the bikini to stroke her smooth brown and white skin and feel the crack in her butt. A surge of mammalian instincts swept over him. He felt that urge to participate directly in human evolution, and his shorts dropped to the floor.

"Yeah baby, that's what the Zen teachers say, nothing special."

*

I meditated some more, and after a while went downstairs and called in through the screen to Cork, who untied himself from Mary, hitched up his shorts, and came to the door.

"Hey man, enough stress," I said through the screen. "I'm sorry Dude, let's go surf Mary Ann's. There's a little waist-to-chest bump over there. I bet it's a ton of fun."

"Happy Times were happy, my friend," Cork retorted with a deadly smile. "That was Zen, this is now. Maybe we shouldn't talk in the morning. Maybe we shouldn't talk at all. You have a stick shoved up your ass about me for some reason, and I don't know why, so go surf Mary Ann's and maybe we'll talk later." Cork slammed the door shut in my face.

I put my longboard in the back of the truck and drove out our street, a skinny one-track lane called *Calle José Perez*, passing Carlito's yellow cement house on the right. Carlito's yard was littered with trash and random dogs and chickens. Mia, his chestnut mare, was tied to a tree in the road. She dutifully pulled in her big backside to let me by. I slowed to a stop and said *"Buen Día"* into her sensitive horsey face and warm brown eyes, and drove north on *Ruta 413* past the central surf breaks of Rincón and over the hill to the other side of *Punta Higuero*. I pulled into the parking lot at Jack's Surf Shack, a ramshackle wooden lean-to and half-truck trailer a few steps from the beach, bought a bar of wax from Jack and paddled out. It wasn't perfect, but it was the day before a new incoming swell, so the leading edge of the pulse was pushing up fun 2 – 3 ft. waves with a very occasional 4-foot set. There was a small tribe of beginners, a paddle-boarder, three longboarders, and one body-boarder. None of them could surf very well. They didn't know where to sit or how to scrimmage for the best waves.

The three longboarders, heavy-set guys, grimaced at everyone like NFL linemen, as if to send the bogus message that they were heavy locals. But it was

soon obvious that these chubby guys were *San Juaneros*, corporate deskmen out to the west side for a break from the office grind. On the last wave of the session I faded left down a steeply sloping 4' face, jammed a right bottom turn into a semi-hollow fast section, ran up to the nose, flew through the breaking section, threw a cutback into the soup, and then swung around to cruise through the last bit of wavelet into the inside reef, knee-boarding up to the sand.

Jack's nickname is Shampoo, a moniker he earned in South Jersey where he cut hair on the go-go bar circuit for the girls working the strip clubs and casinos. Next door to his shop a young surfer couple operate a yoga studio/juice bar out of a bright green truck trailer. Young men and women, several with thick *rasta* dreads, were hanging out around the low cement tables in front of Jack's and the yoga juice bar. A dozen blonde towhead kids ran around in the sand sipping organic juice boxes while their parents passed around a clay pipe, chatting and listening to the Reggae music Jack had racked on his iPod. Shampoo was a large man of Sicilian descent. He and his partner wife Sofia had two kids, Isabela and Luciano. They lived halfway up the hill in an open-air house with fifteen foot ceilings and three giant Great Danes.

"You still want a haircut?" Shampoo asked me.

"Yea, take about this much off," I said, measuring an inch with my thumb and forefinger.

After the haircut, Shampoo took me out back to a small storage area to smoke a private bowl, and then I went next door to the yoga place, got a cup of coffee and a fruit bar, and sat down at a table. Before long a tall woman with shoulder length brunette hair came to Jack's for a haircut, a Californian named Amy Hollingsworth who said she mostly lived in New York, but had just spent a month on the *Isla de Vieques* off Puerto Rico's east coast. I had met her a few nights before at the Calypso bar, and she was fun to talk to. That night, stoned at Calypso, she told me she had two boyfriends in New York, one she loved and one she hated. She said she could easily marry either one of them, but she also assert-ed that monogamy was monotony if it lasted a whole lifetime, positing that most marriages should come with a ten or fifteen year contract, renewable or non-renewable, and the partners should not assume that renewal was an automatic thing.

As Hollingsworth sat there at Calypso sinking further and further into the illuminating veracity of wine and marijuana, she seemed resigned to never marrying either one of her boyfriends and I recognized this as the defining social paradigm of her generation, endlessly deferred matrimony with a pluralistic, poly-amorous, multi-party structure. It was difficult for me to follow the lineaments of this new model precisely, but I was stoned too, so it made perfect sense from a temporal-philosophical point of view; not in the pure Hegelian sense, but more from the Marxist-materialist point of view.

"I had to leave Vieques," Hollingsworth said while Shampoo cut her hair with a lit roach clenched between his teeth. "Too freaky."

"What do you mean?" Shampoo said through a puff of marijuana smoke.

"Everybody's tripping in Vieques. They trip every day. It's like living with aliens. I actually thought they were going to take me to their spaceship and, like, kidnap me to outer space."

"People still do acid there?" I queried.

"No, they forage for psilocybin mushrooms; like we do in Northern California and Oregon... we brought the mushroom thing to Vieques and taught the locals."

"Psychedelic mushrooms – in Vieques?" Shampoo was incredulous. "Jack, they're everywhere up in the hills, if you know where to look. I prefer mushroom tea myself," Hollingsworth added. "It's a body high. I like a body high more than a total head high, but I had to get off island. It was like a fucking Star Wars movie."

During her haircut Amy Hollingsworth was totally unselfconscious, disseminating concise autobiographical reports to Shampoo and me and anyone else within hearing. After an M.F.A. at The New School she moved to San Francisco and worked on a paleo food truck for a couple of years. Then she moved back to

New York, to Williamsburg, Brooklyn, and landed a gig with the Whitney Museum. Her latest plan was to return to California and set-up an organic food truck in Santa Cruz with baked goods, wraps, and a full paleo menu.

*

I was driving home on *Ruta 413* coming down the big hill just before the cow and horse pastures when I felt the transmission on my old Ford Explorer slip out of gear. It had been doing this with a high whining sound on a regular basis, so I shifted into neutral and then slowly slid it back into drive, and the battered old SUV proceeded okay. On the final curve near the end of the cow pasture I saw a young lime green iguana in the other lane, basking in the sun. He was almost in the shoulder of the roadway, which would have been fairly safe, but his long tail was sticking into the lane of potential automobile traffic by a foot or so, so it was possible that he would survive a car coming around the bend. I am not a big fan of iguanas, for several reasons, but in this case I wanted to stop and shoo this juvenile iguana off the roadway. However, just then a carload of clueless tourists came around the bend and there was no way to warn them. The driver was a middle-aged man with both hands on the wheel, itself a dangerous sign, and he was sightseeing, peering up and down at the hills and pastures in all directions as if he had never seen a cow before. I looked in my rear view and spotted the little iguana flipping up and down in the roadway in agony. I stopped, threw the truck into reverse, and backed up twenty yards. There was no blood or guts in the road. That was good. Perhaps only the tail got run over. Maybe he or she could survive a little loss of tail. But then I located the young lizard lying very still in the dry dirt of the shoulder. The latter part of its tail, perhaps the last five inches, was flattened and drained of color, crushed by the tourist car. He was dead. Bled to death.

I drove on and turned into *Calle José Perez*. Carlito's oldest daughter was on the balcony screaming at her mother while Mia grazed quietly in the little field next to the house. In the *marquesina* under the house Carlito and his cousin fiddled with Carlito's '74 Mercury Montego Brougham. Carlito typically wore the fierce expression of Ice-T on his face, but he would wave and smile broadly when I called out, "*Hola, Carlito!*" as I drove by. The *gringo norteamericano* neighbors groused that he never worked a day in his life, and that his family lived on food stamps. Perhaps it was true that Carlito was living off the welfare of the colonial superpower with his food stamp *cupones* and his lifestyle of utter freedom, but I saw some justice in this. After all, shortly after seizing Puerto Rico from Spain in 1898 the American colonial government devalued the Puerto Rican *peso* by 40%, wiping out almost half the middle class's savings and land valuations, and forcing large sectors of the population into bankruptcy. American colonial banks shuttered hundreds of coffee and tobacco plantations that couldn't pay their mortgages, and hundreds of communal food farms and cattle and pig pasturages, replacing them with sugar cane. By 1905 the vast majority of Puerto Rican sugar cane farms were owned by American bank syndicates, including the one owned by the island's first American colonial governor, Charles Herbert Allen, who quit his job after a year to start a sugar syndicate backed by J.P. Morgan Bank. Ex-governor Allen eventually controlled 98% of the sugar processing in the U.S. Today his company is called Domino Sugar.

With their one crop monoculture, Allen and his co-conspirators forced most Puerto Rican farm laborers out of work six months a year (*el tiempo muerto*), ensuring a welfare state ethos for decades to come.

So in my view there is a weird balance of justice in all this, a definitive social praxis in the way that Puerto Ricans like Carlito shun the virtual slave labor that is common in North America. Was this an historical ramification of the old *esclavitud*, the forced *encomiento* labor, the *libreta* system, and America's disastrous management of the Puerto Rican economy?[2] Perhaps this dependence on U.S. welfare and corporate colonialism is a form of subconscious rebellion. I really wonder.

In the *Grundrisse*, commenting on the former slaves of another Caribbean island who refused to work beyond what was necessary for their own subsistence, Marx wrote, "They have ceased to be slaves, . . . not in order to become wage laborers, but, instead, self-sustaining peasants working for their own consumption." It did remind one of the peasant rebellion against government enforced "enclosures" in 18th and 19th century England, when a conspiratorial aristocracy (abetted by a corrupt Parliament in London) seized most of the peasantry's common farm acreage to drive up crop prices and drive down the cost of farm labor.

San Juan metro's capitalist culture sometimes finds the simple *Boricua* life on the farms and hills, and in the villages far from the capital city incomprehen-

---

[2] Slavery, encomiento, and the libreta system were forms of enforced servitude and punitive control of the labor force in Puerto Rico during a span of over 400 years. Today's economy is largely controlled and governed by U.S. federal law, including the jurisdiction of the U.S. House Committee on Natural Resources, whose chairman is the virtual "president" of Puerto Rico.

sible, because unlike life in the capital region, life out "in the island" is not a replica of U.S. suburbia. It is simpler, and more pure. But now San Juan is broke, and morally bankrupt. The central government cannot afford Carlito's *cupones*, and can no longer afford the fact that Carlito works off the books and pays no taxes, working only for himself, his friends, and his family within a close-knit social framework. That was the old *Boricua* way of life far from San Juan. But now the government finds itself in catastrophic debt to U.S. hedge funds and bond-holders, and it is governed by U.S. law, while across the island the small towns and villages continue on as if there were no San Juan. As a thoughtful headline in the island's socialist newspaper asked, "Quién le debe a quién?"[3]

Thursday 19 January

I'm sitting on the couch working on a paper about poets Charles Olson and Philip Whalen for a symposium at the University of British Columbia. During the 1950s and 1960s, through letters and in cross-referential poems, Whalen and Olson conducted a dialogue on the Möbius Strip, a geometric curve with several curious properties. Olson initiated things with his 1946 poem "Möbius Strip," followed by "As the Dead Prey Upon Us" in 1956. In letters back and forth the two poets traded ideas on the geometry and cosmology of "Reimann surfaces" and Möbius strips. It appears that Olson and Whalen were interested in the Möbius strip as a metaphor and geometric representation of human conscious-ness. A line drawn along the length of this geometric closed curve will meet back where it started, but on its "other side," which is really the same side, without ever crossing an edge (finitude). In other words, a line drawn from any beginning point eventually and inevitably returns to its original starting point, as in birth the starting point of human consciousness, and death the end point.

---

[3] "Who really owes who?"

For these poets, it seems to me, the Möbius curve demonstrated (geometrically & metaphorically) how human consciousness could be perceived as having only one unitary boundary, and no duality. Although birth and death appear to the naked eye as two radically different structures, they are really one, and the duality of birth and death is rendered illusory, like the cosmological geometry in last few stanzas of Denise Newman's long poem *The Book of Thel*.

Here is a Möbius strip:

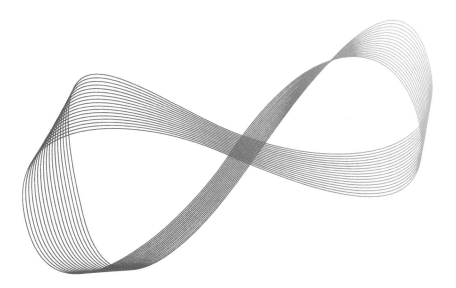

And here is an excerpt from Newman's poem:

> Moving　　the line of the horizon
> rises as I rise, she observes the lines
> of the highway cross at every point
> with lines of eternity.
> [...]
> space expands　　　freely; openly—
> one can pass the huge stone
> at the entrance (conception).

Olson was well aware that Whalen was part of a specifically West Coast group of 'Beat' poets who were heavily influenced by buddhist philosophy, psychology, and ontology, writers like Snyder, Kyger, di Prima, McClure, Albert Saijo and others, who were prone to blend leftist dialectics with a pure existential buddhism. Olson was loathe to leave history and politics out of the equation, so he asked Whalen in correspondence if there was any evidence in the buddhist or Hindu traditions that "any man had so definitely replaced myth by history?"

I saw this as the really good question whether any religion had ever relied on actual material history, rather than myth, as a fundamental philosophical orientation. As usual, Olson came to the big questions with the sheer force of an insubordinate and underivative intellect. Marxism claimed to discard religious mythology unless it was materially utopian in nature, and late capitalism's neo-liberal *weltanschaung* gave Christianity lip service, but not much genuine consideration. Olson was serious about this question. He wasn't really into buddhism like the west coasters, but he had been into politics a few years earlier, serving in the Roosevelt administration during World War II. After the war FDR offered him the chairmanship of the Democratic National Committee, which he turned down to pursue a career as a poet, literary theorist, and teacher. Olson remained interested in public policy at the grass-roots level of the *polis*, the city, the town, in his adopted city of Gloucester, Massachusetts. He developed a 'special view' of history, arguing that history is personal and individual ("it is ourselves and nothing outside us"), not some remote or abstract story separate from ordinary people. I thought this had very cool ramifications for poets, artists, writers, or any philosophically minded person.

I wanted to share these thoughts on Whalen and Olson in my morning seminar, and in the afternoon class stage a discussion on the first few chapters of Hemingway's novel *The Sun Also Rises*. Some scholars consider the character Lady Brett Ashley as a breakthrough feminist figure in early 20th century literature. Lady Brett was based on the real Lady Duff Twysden, who was with Hemingway and his circle in Pamplona during the summer of 1925, when they traveled there from Paris for the bullfights. She was a heavy drinker, fiercely independent of men (while loving them passionately), and according to the feminist scholarship she fucked as many of them as she pleased, a liberated woman. She went to Spain with Hemingway (who was in love with her), her new husband (who was in love with her), and a desperate suitor fictionalized as Robert Cohn (who was in love with her). On arriving in Pamplona she fell in love and had sex with a young, handsome Spanish *toreador*.

Perhaps, I was thinking, the bullfights in Pamplona parallel the meta-culture of the annual surfing competition in Rincón. What is the cultural metaphor embedded in surfing big homicidal ocean waves? Is it the terror associated with the brute, deadly, personless force of nature? Is surfing, in essence, a rebellion against mankind's pitiful de-naturing of the universe? Does it connect with the 19th century 'Romantic sublime' of Wordsworth, Coleridge, and Shelley?

*

The roosters next door screeched, the caged songbirds chirped, and I dozed off, slipping into a dream of Janice. She was in our driveway in New Jersey dressed in black, standing by the rear passenger door of a black Lincoln Town Car. I stood on the porch facing the driveway with my daughters Forrest and

Emily, and my son Carter. The driver of the Town Car wore a white shirt, black tie, and dark suit. He stood motionless by the driver's side door. Janice waved goodbye to me and the kids, her glazing eyes staring out of death.

"She's leaving us," I said. We waved back to her.

"You're coming back on the twenty-fifth, right honey?" I called out, not even knowing what my question meant. Our life together was not completely over? This was just a temporary trip to Hades for her? Janice waved again, staring at us. She opened the passenger door of the black car, got in, and shut the door. The driver got in his side and started the motor. Janice waved one last time, staring through me with sad dark eyes, and a tousle of curly salt and pepper hair. The driver backed out of the driveway and drove up the street until the car disappeared into the trees and houses a few blocks down. I heard Janice's voice say, "You disappear, you disappear from the universe. Just let it go."

A black and orange Puerto Rican oriole flew into the window near the couch where I dreamt, wedging itself between the hurricane slats squawking and shrieking, and I woke up. The oriole glared at me, and then jerked her head around, peering intently at every corner of the room. She fixed her beady eyes on me again, let out an ear-splitting shriek, and flew off into the sky with a stream of bird commentary.

It was almost half past three o'clock. The dream was very real, not like a 'normal' dream. Maybe it was a "revision of categories," where something from the past, like Janice, comes again, as if out of the future. Maybe she is not past but passed; passed by and come again. My mind and perceptions were in an epistemological reversal, turned upside down, as Dōgen does in his writings, in order to understand life in this universe. I thought of the black and orange oriole as a concrete manifestation of Janice because she was a total bird person in real life, saving the birds in our back yard that had been captured by our cats Luke and Lea. She would run out into the yard yelling at Luke or Lea, disentangle the bird from the cat's jaws, and then set the fowl down gently and drag the cat back into the house by the neck folds. Sometimes the bird revived and flew away, other times she would take the wounded creature to the bird doctor lady a few towns over, who patched them up and nursed them back to life. Perhaps the Puerto Rican oriole carried a message from the cosmic bird universe that they cared about Janice, and wanted me to know that.

I went into the kitchen, poured myself a glass of ice-cold chardonnay, and went out and sat on the deck facing the ocean. The air shimmered with an impenetrable silvery light. The sun was so bright that I couldn't even make out the surface of the water. She was out there, somewhere. I could feel it. Then I heard a cat crying on the other side of the house in the front yard, so I walked back through the living room to the narrow balcony facing Don Carlos' pasture. The cat that lived in the pasture, the pretty calico with the classic white, black, and orange markings was sitting in the grass looking up at me. Her eyes were jade discs, dusky, pale as lime juice. I called down to her and she turned and ran into a cluster of fan palms at the end of the driveway. Rory heard me and came out into the front yard. Rory is a tall lanky guy with the sandy blondish hair of the forty-something set.

"Hey, what've you been up to? Haven't seen you since the Cork blow-up," Rory said.

"Nothing much, just working. I've got a few projects past due, just trying to catch up."

"Can I come up?"

"Sure, come on up. I've got some cold chardonnay."

I poured Rory a glass of wine and we sat overlooking the ocean. Rory is one of those people whose intelligence and joy in life manifestly sparkles. Like Janice, he is a very shrewd judge of character. He's always lived in Manhattan surrounded by smart, accomplished people, except for five or six years in Boston, where he co-founded the Boston Gay & Lesbian Alliance.

"You shouldn't have invited Cork up to read that poem," Rory opened with. "His novels are selling, but the only thing he gives a shit about is that poem. He think he's America's answer to Seamus Heaney." I burst out laughing. "Well, who the fuck knows?" I said. "But Seamus Heaney has a heart, and I'm not sure where Cork's got lost. Mary loves him, and she's so great, an incredible woman. But now he has to have Yvonne Acevedo, too. What's that about?"

"Everyone wants Yvonne," Rory responded. "There's no one that doesn't want Yvonne."

"Except maybe you?"

"No," Rory laughed. "I find her sexy too. It's just not my thing. I met a guy I really like last week and I don't want to fuck it up. Anyway, she's all over the map."

"Yeah, and the map leads to Mikey's house in *Barrero*. He's going nuclear over her thing with Cork. They fucking live together."

"And what about you, my friend?" Rory queried. "People wonder when you'll date again." The sky cleared over the ocean and a sheen of orange washed under eggshell clouds on the edge of the horizon.

"Oh, I think I could date... I've tried. It's not easy. I've asked a few people out and they say "no thanks, I'm busy," and then I see them out dancing with their girlfriends. What the fuck?"

"Yeah well, it's not that much better with men. Men are very unpredictable. It's all about their dick, and then it's the money."

"Sounds familiar, not the dick part, the money. Women are legendary about the money thing."

"I'm sorry, but straight men are the worst," Rory asserted. "No criticism of you intended, but I'd rather go out with a really gay guy, or a woman."

"Well yeah, of course. Because you're gay, right?"

"No, it's not even that," Rory said. "I just find that men at a certain age, at 40 or 43, it's just all about who they want to fuck – nothing else. They've already been in love once or twice, so they're over it."

"Aren't gay guys that way too?"

"Just some of them."

*

Rory left after sharing a glass of wine. I realized that if I went to town right away there would be enough time to stop at the print shop and make copies for Monday's classes, then I could make dinner and meet up for drinks with Mary and her friend Monica. Maybe Cork would join us if he had gotten over our little *tête à tête*, maybe not. Leaving the print shop in the *pueblo* I spotted Aidan McClure standing in front of the laundromat with a young woman. His battered '76 Buick *Le Sabre* was parked out front with a quiver of surfboards on top. His woman friend had shiny brown eyes and smooth tan skin. McClure was drinking a can of the local beer, *Medalla*. He had the reckless blonde hair and wise-ass grin of the desperado surfer. The girl was half my age and it was soon apparent that she would not look directly at me. I was a zero, an invisible man, but I wasn't offended. I knew this shit well. There was a critical shortage of single women in Rincón, so older men hit on young women (as well as women their own age) in the vain hope that, statistically speaking, they might succeed in sleeping with someone. I understood the grim statistics well, so I wasn't offended.

McClure's blue eyes drooped under the weight of his sins of the night before. He was grizzled, hung-over, sipping a *Medalla* in the hot afternoon of the day. He didn't introduce me to the brown-eyed girl even though we were standing six inches from each other as she looked off into space, staring at nothing in particular. I knew Aidan's father Patrick from up in Jersey. He was a garrulous, extroverted guy, fun to have a drink with. Pat put Aidan through college on the North Shore of Oahu, and the kid became a fearless charger, attacking Pipe, Sunset, Velzyland, and other top breaks. The surf in Puerto Rico didn't intimidate him. Double-overhead waves were no issue. Triple or quadruple overhead were no problem either; and the more top-to-bottom detonation the better. Aidan could rip anything that slammed into Rincón.

Six or seven soft-top foam surfboards were strapped to the roof of his rusty *Le Sabre*. There had been no real surf for several days, so I concluded that the boards were on his car because he was giving lessons to tourists.

"You give surf lessons?"

"Yeah."

"That's how you make money?"

"Yeah. Everybody's doing it."

"You going to surf the contest next weekend?"

"No, fuck that. I have no respect for that shit."

"Why?"

"The pros will fly in and they'll have jet skis or boats take 'em out. Fuck that. I paddle out."

"You're not going to sign up?"

"Maybe. Depends. If it's gnarly I could wipe out half the pros. They won't know where to hit the ledge."

"What ledge?"

"Dude, you know there's two separate patches of reef on the bottom at Juanita's, right? Think about it. Two main sections off the point. They'll put the contest on the first ledge off the point, and only locals will have the second ledge wired. It's a second peak on the same wave. It throws up in front of you and you back-door it if you have balls, if not you're fucked."

"Maybe you should enter the contest," I said.

"Right. Like I have a hundred bucks for that shit." I watched as they pulled out of the parking lot in the *Le Sabre*, thinking about what Aidan said about the second ledge at Juanita's.

Driving home to cook dinner I decided to stop for a quick drink at Jimmy Bear's Rum Shack, a hotel bar just off the beach. Hank Rosenthal was there, sitting at an outside table with his wife Rachel, nursing a beer. I greeted them and kept on into the bar proper. Hank only permitted himself one beer at a time. We called it the Rosenthal Rule. No one in Rincón had ever seen Hank Rosenthal drink more than one beer. It was a fact of history. Rachel was having a vodka on the rocks *con limón*.

The other odd thing about Hank was that he insisted on giving you a surf report as soon as you ran into him, whether you wanted one or not, and whether it was the topic of conversation or not. I had never asked Rosenthal for a surf report, and I never wanted one. Everywhere you go in Rincón waves are breaking and people are surfing. Surf reports are a waste of time if you can just see it with your own eyes. It is undoubtedly a good thing to know if a new swell is on the way, so you get up in the morning and look at it, and you see the wind direction with your own two eyes, much better than any surf report. As I came into the bar Jimmy greeted me.

"Brendan McGuinness in the house! Brendan McGuinness!" he cried as heads in the bar turned to see who I was. Jimmy was a good conversationalist, and the best New York barman in Rincón. Jimmy was no minimalist. He didn't simply mix his customers drinks, take their money, and then leave them alone so he could dwell in his own head. That was rank minimalism to Jimmy. He was an entertainer, a priest, and a psychologist all rolled into one. He interviewed all the tourists and locals who came into his bar, and he remembered every word they said. A couple would come back a year later from San Juan, or New York, or Maine, or Washington, D.C., and Jimmy would immediately ask them how's the kid doing at Syracuse U., how's the daughter handling the new job in Boston? Is the wife ready to retire yet from Bethpage High School? It was uncanny how many people and how much of their life detail Jimmy could hold in his head. So he was a delight to drink with. Customers came back to the Rum Shack just to see him, season after season, by the dozens, by the hundreds.

Now I sat a few stools down from a Manhattan couple that I vaguely recognized from the year before. Jimmy had told me that the guy owns a hedge fund worth billions, as well as golf courses, luxury hotels, thoroughbred horse farms, etc. He was now based in Puerto Rico as a 'vulture investor' to avoid taxes and make unseemly wealth off the island's sinking finances. Puerto Rico was the latest place, after Detroit and Greece, that the hedge funders were raiding. They come in, buy up distressed debt at cheap prices, and then use corrupt politicians, threats, and coercion to secure massive cash returns.

The hedge funder and his wife were sharply dressed. He had on bright orange shorts, an ice-cream white buttoned down shirt, and powder blue shoes that bespoke more of East Hampton than Rincón. His wife was petite, with jet-black hair cropped short in a page boy. If they had worn ratty shorts and tattered tank tops they might've fit in, but they stood out like rich tourists who landed on the wrong island. Sipping my drink and hearing the hedge funder chat with Jimmy made me think of the television show *Downton Abbey*. Of course it was fiction, but there was a grain of truth in the fact that the Earl of Grantham had a compelling interest in the lives of his employees and in the socioeconomic health of the villagers within his purview. To be sure, he was rich, privileged, and aristocratic, a staunch defender of his class interests, but he also had communitarian impulses, and a fair dose of social compassion. He had received a liberal education at Eton, and then Oxford or Cambridge, and had a decent library at home. He could get through a difficult book and carry on an intelligent conversation about it, if need be.

I knew it was unfair of me, but I couldn't help but compare the wealthy Wall Streeters I knew with the Earl of Grantham. They were empty windbags compared with the Earl. Why couldn't the fucking Americans make an effort to obtain a respectable education in the liberal arts and humanities? Could any of them read a decently complex book? It is so depressing how ignorant most of them are. You go to their houses and all you see is giant flat-panel TV's and bookshelves full of shitty book-of-the-month club titles.

I left Jimmy a generous tip, said good night to the hedge fund and his wife (who were actually very kind and polite to me), and I was on my way out the door when I spotted Mikey 'Surf' Bellamy sitting at a table behind a low masonry wall. Mikey owns the bar called *La Casa Vieja* in a little alley off the back side of town. It's hard to find, but it's a good bar with very good music. Mikey was sitting alone with a double white rum on the rocks. He was unshaven and nastily hung-over with his black-rimmed glasses, stubbly red beard and short-cropped dark reddish hair. He looked bloody awful, smoking an American Spirit cigarette; his eyes blasted with bright pink blood vessels.

"Hey Brendan, come over here," Mikey called to me. "I've been looking for you."

"What's up, Mikey?" I said.

"I want to talk to you, man," he said in a gravelly alcoholic slur.

"I miss Janice."

"I do too Mikey, but let's not start on this again, okay? I've got my own problems."

"Dude, you were lucky to get that girl, you know that, right?"

"I know, Mikey. You already told me that. Do you really want to have this conversation again, because I don't."

"She was too good for you, Brendan. You're a fucking asshole sometimes."

"Sure, whatever, Mikey."

"Okay, okay sport. Chill out. How're your classes going?"
"Not bad I guess, a lot of work."

"I hope you're teaching these kids to fuck the bullshit."

"Tryin'."
Mikey motioned to the waitress for a round of drinks.

"I haven't eaten in three days."

"Mikey, you have to eat. You're drinking too much. People say you're getting drunk at work and giving half the bar away. You're going to lose your business."

"Yeah, well, I *am* fucked up. Yvonne is cheating on me. We're breaking up. Back in the day when I needed someone to talk to, I had Janice. I could talk to her. We'd ride our bikes down the beach to Belmar or Spring Lake and back, talking the whole way. You couldn't even ride with her a few blocks to West End and back."

"I know, Mikey, I'm sorry. I should've. I just don't like bikes."

"Yeah, but you could've just taken a fuckin' bike ride with her." Tears formed in Mikey's eyes. I clenched my lips to control an upwelling of emotion.

"You make me feel like shit, Mikey."

"You know what I dug the most about her?" Mikey continued. "No one could bullshit her. I bullshit everybody, not her."

Mikey knew the truth. I should have spent more time with E-E after she got sick, but I could never ever accept the fact that she would become sicker and sicker and die. It was too heavy. I couldn't deal with it. She knew the odds. Oncologists were career liars, glorified undertakers. She had a handle on death. She knew it was coming.

"You always make me feel like shit, Mikey," I said. Mikey took a pull on his American Spirit.

"I'm sorry man. I'm just fucked up. Yvonne's breaking up with me and I got no one to talk to."

"I'm a good listener, Mikey. I'll come to the bar, we can talk."

"No, you're a shitty listener, Brendan. You're too uptight. Who wants to talk to you? Don't you notice that people don't want to talk to you? You're a fuckin' time bomb with a stick shoved up your ass."

"No, Cork's the time bomb. People talk to me all the time, Mikey. You talk, I'll listen. I'm a good listener."

"You suck as a listener, Brendan. You *pretend* to listen, and your friend Cork's an asshole. He and Yvonne are fucking and I haven't even moved out of the house yet! Why do you hang out with such assholes, Brendan? Nobody can understand that about you. You have no fucking immunity to assholes."

"Cork and I grew up together, Dude. We're friends. You can't always choose your friends."

"That pig Cork O'Reilly... you think he could've waited a decent month or two? It's not enough that he's fucking Mary. He has to fuck Yvonne, too? What is it with you Irish guys? You have to fuck everyone?"

"No I don't, Mikey. I can't even get a date. I didn't even really know about Cork and Yvonne. You told me she was going to have a thing with Hank."

"That's what Hank thought, but now Cork's in and Hank's out. And I'm sleeping on the fucking back porch with Road Kill!"

"Look, here comes Hank."

Hank and Rachel Rosenthal were making their way over to Mikey and Brendan's table.

"What an asshole," Mikey said under his breath as Hank came closer. "Don't ask him for a surf report. See what he does."

"Hey what's up, you guys surf today?" Hank asked, pulling up chairs for himself and Rachel. "I caught Domes this morning three to six feet, four people out. It went off all morning. Where were you guys?"

"Hank, I didn't ask you for a surf report," Mikey barked. "I was just telling Brendan what an asshole you are, and now you're here, so I'll tell you myself." Hank blanched and said, "What are you talking about, Mikey?" Mikey looked over at Rachel. She was a small-boned woman with a nicely crafted Eastern European face and dark curly hair.

"Rachel, I'm sorry you have to hear this because I like and respect you, but your husband has been trying to fuck my wife Yvonne."

"Oh cut it out, Mikey," Hank pleaded. "I never tried a thing with Yvonne. I barely know her, and Rachel and I have always treated you with respect. So why do you have to make shit up and rag on me all the time?"

"Dude, my wife is kicking me out of the house and half the guys in town aretrying to fuck her, including you, so I hope Rachel kicks your sorry ass. And tell me this Hank, why do you worry so much about your status in this shit town, and two, why can't you drink more than one fuckin' beer with us? It drives people fucking crazy."

Hank was stunned. Rachel stayed calm. She was more disturbed that Hank had publicly embarrassed her than the fact that he had the hots for Yvonne Acevedo. After all, she reasoned, Yvonne is extremely attractive and Hank's a guy.

"I don't *want* to drink, Mikey," Hank continued, "that's why I don't drink. Look what it's done for you. Look in a mirror. You should check into an alcohol program. Why would I want to get as fucked up as you?"

"I'll tell you why, Hank," Mikey shot back. "Because I have standing in this community and you don't, even with your big house up the hill and your disgusting fucking BMW. All you have is money, ego, and that shitty fucking blog. And if you just once let go of your bullshit, got wasted with us, and lived in our flip-flops for a day or two, you might like it. You might walk away from that tiny fuckin' micro-verse where you're the king – I may be a drunk, Hank, but I own a bar where men and women drink, and I have more going on in here than you ever will," Mikey said, pointing to his heart.

The blood vessels in Mikey's face pulsated with the quantum of rum running through his veins. Hank was overwhelmed, speechless. No one had ever confronted him with such blunt truths about himself. Rachel shifted in her seat. Later she told me that it was basically true, Hank was always busy crafting his public persona, not only in social media, but even in the most mundane everyday conversations with people. It was non-stop PR. She mentioned that she had been re-reading Fredric Jameson lately, and that she had two classes with him at Duke when she was an undergraduate. What Jameson said was sometimes difficult to follow, but he was deadly accurate. Reputation and person as one? That was just one more example of the social pathology of late capitalism... the hypostatized 'person,' a player in a game. They can't be one, Rachel remonstrated with me, the inner core of self-being and the outer, illusory reputation-person? No way. The inner self, is being itself, the *ding an sich*, it can't be just another fetishized commodity... if there is to be any real freedom. Jameson was so right. Mikey's drunken blasts had core validity.

"I'm sorry you feel like this about me, Mikey," Hank finally said. "I'll try to do better for you."

"No, do better for Rachel," Mikey fired back. "Be a man, not a fucking press release from hell."

There was a pregnant silence. The Caribbean air was moist and thick. Hundreds of tiny *coqui* frogs chirped in the trees, singing "*Coqui, coqui, coqui!*" The silliness of their sing-song added a sense of absurdity to the situation. I didn't think of Hank as a bad guy. He was basically a good guy, it was just weird that he thought of himself as a surfing legend because he raised money for shi-shi causes in L.A. and East Hampton. And yes, it was weird that he never really drank or got high with us guys. That's how men in Rincón bonded, and some of the women too. It was part of the culture. I was thinking that Hank could come with us to Mikey's bar, have a few drinks with us, chill out. We could toke a joint on the way over. Mikey would ease up on him, and we'd all be friends again. Everything would be okay.

"Mikey, take it easy on Hank," I finally said. "Don't break his balls. He's a good guy. He does a lot with Surfrider Foundation and stuff. Let's get out of here and smoke a bowl and chill at *Casa Vieja*. Hank, come with us, we'll drop Rachel off at the house and go to Mikey's bar. He's just upset. He's going through a lot. Yvonne's kicking him out and he's sleeping on that shitty porch with the dog. And Rachel, Mikey doesn't really think Hank was hitting on Yvonne. He's just breaking balls, really."

"Rachel, what do you say?" Mikey growled. "Can your guy come out and have a few beers with us?"

"Of course he can, Mike," Rachel answered, "after I kill him he can do whatever he wants."

Now the ball was in Hank's court. His choices were clear, go out with the guys, or go home to his ego palace. Hank could have passed the litmus test right then and there and been admitted back into Mikey Surf's graces, but he was afraid to get high on beer and weed, afraid that the random anarchy of the universe might encircle him, and he wouldn't be able to operate from the safety of his master control booth.

"I can't," Hank said, looking at his watch. "The kids are up at the house and Rachel is finishing up her drink… I promised I'd take her home."

*

Mikey was too drunk to drive, and we couldn't stop at *La Casa Vieja* because his customers would see him piss drunk and he would buy drinks for everyone in the bar three times over. Also, it was rare, but technically possible, that he might get stopped for a D.U.I. (drunk driving offense). That had never happened in Rincón to anyone's knowledge. The local cops didn't even have breathalyzers. Still, it seemed at least a remote possibility. Jimmy Bear always said that in order to get arrested for drunk driving in Rincón you had to get into an accident with a patrol car, as he had some years back, on the beach road. Lucky for him the cop he sideswiped was one of his best customers at the Rum Shack, Benny Pacheco. Benny let Jimmy go with a friendly warning.

We drove along the beach road taking drags on a roach Mikey found in the ashtray, and rolled into the *pueblo* with its big Roman Catholic and Presbyterian churches on either end of the square. *Los Hermanos* restaurant facing the square has crisp *pollo fritura* and fresh salty *papas fritas*, as well as very good pizza. A clutch of old men were sitting out front in little chairs sipping *Cerveza Medalla*. It was nearly eleven o'clock, and they were taking in the night air, having fun, drinking beer, talking and laughing at their own jokes. An expensive brew pub had opened next door to *Los Hermanos* and a knot of American tourists and corporate *San Juaneros* were clustered around the pub's high tables drinking fancy craft beers.

"You go in, I'm drunk," Mikey said, handing me a twenty dollar bill.

"No, I got it," I said.

Tomás Cabrera, a student from my afternoon class, was working behind the counter. He was a quiet, sensitive kid who turned in well-written, thoughtful assignments.

"*Hola Tomás, ¿comó estás*?" I said.

"*¡Professor! Bien, gracias. ¿Qué quieres?*

"*Dame dos piezas de pollo fritura*," I replied, pointing to a tray of fried chicken legs attached to big triangular shoulder joints, "*y una bolsa de papas fritas.*"

"How are the Hemingway readings going for you so far, Tomás?"

"Oh, pretty good," Tomás replied, scooping hot French fries into a paper bag for me. "I like the descriptions of Spain. My family is from Spain and I have never seen a bullfight, but to tell you the truth, I really want to see one." I mentioned to Tomás something I read in one of Allan Weisbecker's books.

"Some people compare bullfighting to surfing – you know, the raw confrontation with nature that can kill you."

"That's interesting, professor. I will look into that."

"If you want to write about it let me know. I'll take one bottle of Heineken, *también*, Tomás. *Todo para llevar.*"

I paid and left through the open door into the coolness of the street. Mikey was standing alongside the car smoking a cigarette, staring at the tourists.

"You see those kids at the yuppie bar?" Mikey said.

"Sure, what about them?"

"They'll spend nine or ten dollars on a yuppie beer, but they won't walk next door to *Los Hermanos* for a one dollar slice of pizza or four dollars for a dinner of *pollo, arroz y habichuelas*. Fuck them."

" Okay Mikey, chill."

We drove through town taking slugs from the icy Heineken bottle, shoving our hands into the bag of salted fries. Mikey took out another cigarette and lit it with his lighter.

"Do you mind?"

"Nah, go ahead, this once anyway." He took a deep drag and blew cigarette smoke out into the streets of the *pueblo*. People were walking here and there, a few bars were open. Men were playing dominos alongside the Presbyterian Church under the painting of Jesus. Mikey took another drag and exhaled.

"Bro, I totally busted Yvonne and Cork."

"What are you talking about?"

"I caught her lying. She told me she was going to San Juan for an art show or a gallery opening or something, but she went to New York with Cork."

"Yeah I remember you told me she was going to San Juan."

"It was all bullshit. She went to New York. I had Tom the Jet Blue flight attendant check the passenger manifests. She flew straight to JFK with Cork. Tom even gave me the row and seat numbers."

"Jesus, you're like the C.I.A. Tom could get fired. I hope Jet Blue doesn't catch him."

"Tom's my brother, Brendan. I would never let him get hurt. Besides, Yvonne was my wife. This is really fucked up. We could've worked it out but these asshole friends of yours are trying to fuck her."

"I'm sorry, Brah." Mikey's words slid out soaked in rum. He had a bizarre clarity of mind when he was drunk; it could be difficult to follow his train of thought and logic, etc., but he was always highly intelligent.

"Dude, I loved Janice," Mikey said. "Yvonne and I slept together, paid the bills, went places, but it wasn't real love – not like what you had with Janice, and I could have had."

"You sure you want to go there, Mikey? Some things you just leave alone, man. Keep it private. You loved her, I loved her. It's all cool now."

"Dude, you better not be referring to sex, because my relationship with your wife was pure Platonic, no sex. Jesus, you're so hung up on sex, and it's so goddamn pathetic! Why don't you ever grow up, Brendan? That's all she ever wanted from you. Just grow up!"

I didn't say anything. Curls of gray smoke slithered out of the Explorer into the moist air. Mikey's skin glistened. Beads of sweat collected over his brow. I kept my eyes on the road. We passed the last bar in town, then the *estadio municipal*, and turned right into *Barrio Barrero*. Mikey continued, "Pull over, I have to piss. And I gotta tell you something now or I never will... pull over, we'll finish the joint."

I pulled over on the shoulder and turned the engine off. Mikey got out, took a piss in the grass and got back in. He pulled the roach out of the ashtray and lit it. Sweet-smelling marijuana smoke filled the truck.

"You sure you want to tell me this, Mikey? I don't mind if you want to keep anything secret."

"Brendan, I want you to understand something. You're uptight all the time, with your books, your Jameson, your Marxism, your Zen Buddhism, and all that other intellectual crap no one cares about. Janice didn't give a shit. She liked your books too, but she and I know everything you know without reading your goddamn books.... We see it all, Dude! And she'll never come back here again, my friend. She might be spinning around in space in some weird dimension we can't even see, but you and I will never know it, and we'll never see her with these eyes. So, confession time. I wanted to have an affair with your wife and I'm sorry; I'm really, really sorry. I'm a shitty friend, a traitor. But the truth is, Brendan, it could never happen." Mikey was crying softly now.

"She said we couldn't do it, it would fuck things up, we should all just stay friends. She loved you, Dude. I loved her. She loved me. What the fuck." Tears rolled down Mikey's cheeks.

I already knew all this. Janice told me everything, so it didn't really matter. She was that rare person who just naturally took in the whole universe, leaving nothing out. I stared out the window into the dome of sky overhead. She was out there somewhere, I don't care what anybody says. What Mikey said didn't bother me. People's desires and emotions are beyond their own reach. That's what she used to say, and it's true. I started up the truck. Mikey calmed down.

We rounded a bend. The *Barrero* sea glittered under the moonlight. The road was hilly, winding up and down.We pulled in Mikey's driveway. Road Kill was asleep on the front porch. He jumped for joy when Mikey unlatched the front gate. Janice had saved Road Kill's life a few years back, pulling him off the road and nursing him back to health after some heartless idiot threw him out of a moving car on the *Rio Culebrinas* bridge. So Mikey named him Road Kill.

Mike & Yvonne's place in *Barrero* was filled with tropical plants, ferns, art work and hundreds of pulp fiction paperbacks in neat rows on wooden book-shelves, seedy detective stories about guys with guns and edgy women who liked to screw them. Mikey also had two or three hundred classic vinyl albums, including a dozen or so retro surf discs from the 1950s and 60s, very rare LP's. When E-E was alive we would drive to Mikey and Yvonne's, smoke a joint, watch a movie, drink beers, put on music, and talk all night. Sometimes Mikey would say something about life, literature, or buddhism that I disputed, and it really pissed him off. Maybe I thought he came to his conclusions too easily, too broadly. I mean, he was a beach boy from Hermosa Beach, California, a former punk rocker at CBGB's on the Bowery in the East Village. He didn't give a shit about intellectual consistency, and why should he?

Mikey found it frustrating not to be recognized as an artist, or at least as a fine critic of American culture – a film, music, or literary critic – and the absence of broad public endorsement of his opinions on American film, literature, and music really bothered him. It was palpable, and he required his friends to affirm his vision unreservedly. Janice never disputed him on these topics, nor did his longboarder buddy, Rocket Rob. Rocket Rob was remarkable in this respect. He gave Mikey whatever he needed, whenever he needed it. He endorsed everything Mikey said, reaffirming Mikey's aesthetic and philosophical opinions on every topic, whether it was religion, politics, film, music, or literary. Rocket Rob was a very good friend. Mikey could say anything, and Rocket Rob always just smiled in agreement, like a big chubby Buddha.

Mikey calmed down and rolled a fresh joint. We sat out on the back deck with Road Kill. Who gives a shit? I thought to myself. Rocket Rob has it down. Just give people what they want. That's all they care about. They don't care about anything else. No one gives two shits about intellectual consistency, and no one knows anything particularly special that the rest of us don't know. Look at oncologists, well-paid liars. Mikey was right. I should not be so uptight. I was definitely too uptight. Everyone is already enlightened, that's true Dōgen Zen. Everything important to know is right there in front of us. Just scratch the surface.

　　We smoked the joint. Road Kill got stoned too. The three of us sat on the deck under the sextillion million universe of stars while the lights of the city of Mayagüez twinkled in the distance. The midnight ferry to the Dominican Republic slid by lit up like a birthday cake. We talked late into the night. I agreed with everything Mikey said. It was easy. I don't remember passing out but in the morning I woke up on the ratty couch. Mikey was curled up in a sleeping bag on the floor. I went home and changed, and drove to the university for my classes.

B &W
NOTEBOOK 4

Love stains, love pains.

Amerigo Mackeral

B&W Notebook 4

Sunday 22 January, 2012

Toward evening I took out a thick red Angus steak from the refrigerator, cut it in half, sliced and minced garlic and onions and marinated the steak in a thick Merlot gravy, with salt and pepper, hot local salsa, and a dollop of Jamaican barbecue sauce. Coming down the stairs to the grill in the back yard I saw that the plump white rabbit under the house next door now shared its prison cage with a large black and red rooster. The rabbit had its back turned on the rooster, who was the penal intruder; two totally different species forced to live, breathe, eat, and defecate within inches of each other. One cage over two fat black and white songbirds looked up at me with mournful eyes, perched on a high mound of their own shit.

Down in the yard with a glass of ice-cold chardonnay in hand I lit the grill. It was set up alongside a round cement picnic table with a little shed roof over it. Beyond the back fence clean 4 -5-foot sets were roping into the beach. The swell was building. I poured organic wood and vegetable charcoal into a metal funnel on the bottom grate of the grill, lit the newspaper at the bottom of the funnel, and when the coals were red hot removed the funnel, poured the coals onto the top grate, and let them cool down until they were ripe for grilling.

The broad expanse of sky was tinted red and orange for a thousand miles in each direction. I sipped chardonnay as the charcoal baked and the sun dropped further, throwing a rumble of orange over the hills. Seeing the fire move along quickly, I went back upstairs, cut chunks of jumbo farm carrots, battered them in olive oil, salt, and basil, and put them in the oven on a high heat. The temperature knob had broken off so I set the heat level with a pair of pliers, re-filled my glass with Malbec, and poured some over the steak. I took sliced vegetables out of the refrigerator and made two vegetable skewers. On one I placed pungent chunks of onions and red and yellow peppers seasoned with garlic and grainy black pepper flakes. The other I loaded up with wide, flat porcini mushrooms dripping in olive oil. Then I gathered everything, including a pincer tool for grilling and a knife and fork, and went down to the fire.

It was several minutes past peak flame and the heat of the fire pressed against my belly as I placed the skewers on the far side of the grill and the two halves of steak in the middle, over the hottest point. I sprinkled a finely hand-crafted garlic powder from Italian Brooklyn over everything, plus crunchy sea salt, and fresh ground pepper. I ran up and got the carrots out of the oven and threw them on the grill for a minute or two. After another minute it was time to take the steaks off before they got too well done.

Just at that moment, stoned and no doubt half-drunk, Cork O'Reilly came stumbling down *Calle José Perez* past the white and yellow stucco houses and the horse and cow pastures of Don Carlos and his son Carlito. His paunch sagged over his shorts, and his salt & pepper hair blew about in the trade winds. "Everything here moves so fast," he cogitated in his stupor, "insects, birds, clouds, the wind; everything moves so fast. That's why Puerto Ricans move so slow, because everything else around them moves so fast." As I poured him a glass of wine and made him a dish of food Cork asserted that this latter "penetrating insight" into the speed of things in Puerto Rican culture was a sign of his brilliance, a brilliance that would one day elevate him to the ranks of a Frank McCourt, or a Seamus Heaney. Maybe so, I thought to myself. "Who knows?" The sun was now perched on the lip edge of the horizon and the sky suddenly went blue-gray, and the surface of the ocean turned black. Shafts of yellow fire shot up around the sinking disc.

I told Cork I really wanted to check out his Kerouac poem, and that I would send it along to the poetry editors of Zen Monster. He jumped up, grabbed me around the neck, and planted a kiss on top of my head.

"I know you think of me as a dumb ass, but I see shit too, Brendan. I have depth, Brah. When I get back to New York I'm going to that zendo on 23rd Street and I'm getting back with those guys Kōshin and Chodo. They said I can do a *sesshin* with them in March. I need it, Brendan. I need to chill out, do more *zazen*. There's just too much going on in my life, man, too much emotional crap."

"Wow, that's good to hear, Cork. I hope you do that *sesshin* with Kōsho."

"Yeah, we've been emailing and texting."

"I think going back to Zen practice might be good for you," I said, half-kidding, "because lately you've been like the opposite of a buddhist, right?"

"That's my point with you man!" Cork exclaimed. "You are *so* dualistic, and dualism is so uncool. Kerouac saw right through it. That's why he drank himself to death."

"Dude, dualism had nothing to do with Kerouac's alcoholism," I replied.

"It's a disease. He's not some kind of great buddhist because he drank himself to death."

"Oh, so he can't be enlightened because he drank, is that what you're saying? What about Trungpa? Was he crazy or enlightened, or just crazy-enlightened? The buddhists refuse to talk about this stuff. And what about that Zen teacher in Santa Cruz, Kobun Chino, Steve Jobs' teacher. He was a big drinker and a very cool dude. Was he enlightened? Listen to what he said in a lecture once. It goes something like this. I memorized it:"

> We sit in meditation to make life meaningful; the significance
> of life is not realized when you are striving to create some perfect
> thing. Just start with accepting yourself, who you are. Sitting *zazen*
> brings us back to who we are, where we are. So much of the time
> we don't even know who we are, or where we are. We can't see.
> Zen practice is the candle in our darkest room.

That was very cool, what Cork recited from Kobun. I knew Kobun Chino was a really cool guy, a rebel too. When I lived out west I knew some people who knew him. People like Michael Wenger, David Chadwick, Blanche Hartman. They really dug Kobun, too. It was either Chadwick or Mike Wenger who told me that Kobun couldn't tolerate the priestly hierarchy and related nonsense that came to dominate much of American Zen. He didn't like the bullshit, and the bullshit just kept getting bigger and bigger. Still, Kobun remained part of the wider Zen community. He was a very cool dude.

"Okay, what's your answer," Cork queried me, "are you saying Kobun and Trungpa Rinpoche were not enlightened, or just that they had a karmic problem?"

I had to think a minute. I hadn't really thought about this topic very much. Then I remembered the Fox Kōan. Everyone has karma, every human being. So even enlightened Zen teachers have karma to deal with, even buddhas. As Norman Fischer once said, "No people, no buddhas." Karma is a human universal, an historical universal, because remember, Shakyamuni Buddha was a human being in history. No one escapes their karma entirely, unless perhaps at death. Now I was ready to answer Cork's question.

"Okay sure, yeah, they were enlightened, whatever that means. But they had karmic issues they couldn't get over. I've seen patches of ignorance or stupidity in almost every great Zen teacher I've had. And yet they were excellent teachers, the best. That's why it's better for your teacher to live on the other side of the mountain from you. So you don't see their petty faults too often."

"Nice answer, B," Cork said. "Now what's eating you? You're constantly breaking my balls lately. What's it all about?"

"What do you mean?"

"Nothing I do is good enough. My buddhism sucks, my novels suck, my poem sucks. Everything I do is wrong, and everything you do is right. You invite me up for coffee to read my poem and when I get upstairs you say, "It's too early Cork you fuckin' idiot, what the fuck are you doing interrupting my writing and meditation, and while you're at it keep Mary and her stupid friends quiet. It's insulting, man!"

"I'm really sorry, Corky. I fucked up this morning."

"You told Rory that his boyfriend's job at *GQ* is meaningless capitalist bullshit, some crap about "bourgeois *commodification*" and 'late' capitalism." You're lucky Rory doesn't get pissed off like me." A small grin stole across my face, but Cork wasn't amused.

"You think it's funny?! You with the bourgeois university job? You bitch about meaningless bourgeois shit every day, Brendan! When's *Chegüí* cutting the grass? When's *Chegüí* doing the recycling? When's Rosa cleaning the house?" Some fucking Marxist!" Cork was all charged up, pacing around, waving his arms up and down.

"I don't know anyone in this town with more servants than you. And then, when we have a normal disagreement about something, you say if I don't agree with you we don't have to talk! What the fuck, Brendan! You're the only person who's read a book! Rory graduated fucking Georgetown *summa cum laude*, what did you manage at Brooklyn College, a B+ average? Now you have a Ph.D. and we're all stupid kooks?!"

"I'm sorry man, I... "

"Dude, you need to do a serious *sesshin* this year! You have a lot of shit to get out of your system, Brah. We're waiting for you to move on, my brother!"

It was true that I had been tough on Cork for months now, and it had to do with Janice. It was bitter, burning inside me. I had to get it out. Cork had been an unmitigated, unrepentant asshole to her when she was alive. He was prideful, selfish, bombastic, solipsistic; doing cocaine and drinking to the point of repugnance. He fathered no children but tried to cultivate an avuncular bond with our daughter Forrest while being an intolerable asshole to me and Janice on and off for ten years, routinely insulting her for no apparent reason. Yet, in spite of his offensive rudeness, I knew that Cork was deeply loyal to me, and that deep inside he had a good heart, and was a good person. He just didn't know how to express it.

"Okay, you want to hear it, buddy?" I asked him.

"Yeah, what is it Laddy?"

"Janice."

"Motherfucker," Cork said.

Cork felt this coming, walked to the back fence, and gazed at the soft blackness of sea. He and Janice were opposites and they detested each other. I loved them both, stuck in the middle. While E-E preferred quiet gestures, intimate conversations, and was not entirely comfortable in the drinking life of the pub, Cork loved only the pub. He was loud and boisterous and at any pub or dinner party he was either a polarizing or entertaining figure. Sometimes both at the same time. He never had a relationship with a woman lasting more than four or five months, except now with Dr. Mary North, his longest relationship so far. Janice, on the other hand, had just two love relationships spanning her entire lifetime, her two husbands. The first, Greg, for ten years and then twelve years with me; and she took emotional and spiritual care of both of us right up to the very end.

Unlike Cork, Janice didn't distribute herself across a wide social spectrum in pubs, cafés, social media, or other venues. She was a 4th grade teacher in a poor Afro-Haitian ghetto, and aside from her husband and children, her sisters and nieces, and the cats, dog, and birds within her purview, she cared most about the kids in her classroom, their home life, and how she might help them. Her circle was small and tightly woven, mostly (but not only) Jewish and Italian, and when she let you in you soon realized that you had entered into relations with a naturally wise human being, a rare human being, a person without conceit and with no plans for social advancement. She was the kind of person that made you felt better about yourself just being around her; rare, compelling, and highly humorous. I walked over to Cork at the back fence.

"When Janice died, a few months later I went to Miami to give a paper and I got drunk with a young English professor. She was a nice person, and I was really tempted to sleep with her. I needed something. Janice's death made me insane. No one knew how insane I was. I resisted sleeping with that woman to respect Janice and when I told you about it you said I fucked up, that I should have slept with her. Your comment was, "Don't worry about it buddy, you could've done better than Janice. Now you can get someone really hot, like you always wanted."

The last light folded under the horizon. The hills went dark. Cork was speechless, looking out over the water. I bit my lip to stop tears from falling out. I had allowed my best friend to treat my wife like shit, and now she was dead. There was no recuperation, no recompense for this. I had tolerated intolerable bullshit.

"You're going to be a buddhist now, buddy? You've got a long way to go,"

I said. Cork didn't respond. He walked over to the picnic table, picked up some dishes, and took them upstairs, stepping over the corpse of a tiny field mouse on the front patio. Thousands of Puerto Rican ants swarmed over the dead mouse. I went up and washed dishes while Cork retreated to the living room to watch NFL highlights on TV. After a few minutes he walked to the kitchen doorway.

"Dude, I'm sorry. I am an asshole. I've always been an asshole. Most of the time I just want people to think about me; center of attention. I know I broke Janice's balls. I don't know why, I just did it. I think I was jealous of her, and I wanted to see if I could piss her off. I'm sorry man. It's on me."

"Yeah well, you did piss her off. . . everybody fucks up sooner or later,

and you really fucked up. You were cruel to us and I'm like, your best friend."

"I didn't mean that about you getting a hot chick after Janice. I said it to hurt you, because I'm jealous. What are my fuckin' relationships, three months, six months tops? I'm such a fuckin' loser when it comes to women. Now I've been with Mary a year and it's falling apart."

"Yeah, well, cheat on people and relationships fall apart, duh… let's go out for a drink. I gotta get out of the house."

"Yeah, we'll walk down to Yico's. Mary's there with her friend Monica. Monica's pretty hot, maybe you'll get laid finally." Cork walked back to the living room and turned up the volume on the TV. He packed some grass into a little ceramic pipe on the coffee table, and lit it up. Sweet marijuana smoke poured out the top.

"Not me, no sex," I called out from the kitchen. He walked the pipe into the kitchen and I took a hit.

"Trust your wing man, Dude. We'll bring the girls back here to smoke a bone and after a half-hour Mary and I will split, leaving you alone with Monica. Dude, it's a lock." He went back out to the living room to watch football analysts in expensive suits spout bullshit about the NFL post-season now in its final weeks. I stood in the doorway drying a dish. "So what is it with you and Mary? I thought you guys had a good thing going, and then you start an affair with Yvonne Acevedo? What's that supposed to mean, Mr. Buddhist? Mikey Surf is really pissed at you. He and Yvonne fucking live together. They're practically married."

Cork had to think. He took another hit on the pipe and turned up the volume on the remote. The ESPN anchor was sitting at a bright blue plastic desk blabbing away, erroneously predicting how the Baltimore Ravens would destroy the Pittsburgh Steelers in Saturday's play-off game. A sickly montage of fake plastic colors flashed all around him like a circus show.

"Mikey's always pissed about something," Cork retorted. "That red-haired fuck needs to go on the wagon. Yvonne can't take it anymore. Who can live like that? The guy's drunk all the time."

"And what about you and Mary?"

"Mary's about to fire my ass anyway. She's moving to Philadelphia for a medical fellowship, *plus* she has the hots for that dude who works at Shampoo Jack's. The kid's fifteen years younger than me, Brendan. I'm pre-empting her next move. It's strategic. You wouldn't understand." I went back into the kitchen to dry off silverware and wine glasses.

"And don't try to set me up with Monica. I'm still too fucked up over Janice," I called out.

"MacDuff!" Cork said, "you and Monica alone, under the stars. She's hot, man, she's single, and she's on vacation!"

"I'm not into it."

Cork got up and came back to the kitchen doorway with the pipe in one hand and his glass of Malbec in the other, eyes blazing with wine and marijuana.

"My brother, we're going to work on your problem this month," Cork declared. "I'm channeling Janice now. She's whizzing around up there in space, looking down at you and you know what she's saying to me? She's saying, "Corky, I know you're an asshole, but help my guy move on! It's been almost three years! Help my guy move on, Brah!" I looked over at Cork from the sink. "Anyone ever tell you you're a fucking lunatic?" We left for Yico's Nautico Bar. Walking down the stairs I pointed out the fat brown rabbits huddled in the tight prison cages underneath the house next door, the black and white song birds living on their own shit, and the plump white rabbit stuck in a tiny prison cage with her despised roommate, the black and orange rooster. We stopped to look at them.

"Look at these poor creatures," I said quietly. "They call animal husband-ry a hobby, so why do they have to humiliate them? Rabbits like their own rabbit people. They hate fucking chickens."

"How do you know?"

"Dude, it's obvious. Look at them." The rabbit had his back turned on the rooster with a look of disgust on her furry face. Cork surveyed the hu-

man-created landscape of filth, fear, and loathing. "Brendan, you need to come over here in the middle of the night, cut the cages, and set my people free," he said. "The time for revolution is now."

We crossed over the mouse at the bottom of the stairs, its bones now picked clean by the busy ants and its internal organs totally eviscerated. The mouse's eye sockets were licked clean, devoid of flesh. We went out the back gate onto the beach, weaving in and out in the thick sand between the coral rocks strewn in our path. Cork scraped his toe on a sharp one, cursing loudly. We continued on a few yards and came up off the beach down a path to Yico's. The young barman Johnny G, Jr. was behind the stick. I ordered a *Don Q Limón* on ice with a splash of *jugo de piña* and a wedge of lime. Cork asked Johnny for a *Ron del Barrilito* neat, with a peel of lemon.

Johnny G was a second generation barman in Rincón. His father had been a highly respected *caballero* back in the days when the first American surfers began to arrive in the 1960s. Ex-pats who had been in Rincón a long time remembered Johnny G, Sr. well. He was *un hombre de respeto*, a very cool dude, and they passed on that respect to his son, and to his wife Lydia.

Johnny G's family worked the sugar cane plantations in and around Rincón for generations, celebrating Caribbean life in their simple *bohios*, surviving 400 years of Spanish greed, brutality, and racism with pluck and resilience; and now 100 years of American colonial rule. Their predicament in a tropical paradise evolved into the *Boricua* way of living, a devotion to the simple but profound joys in life that no one can take away, not even powerful governments in strange and distant capitals. Young Johnny G had the broad smile of his people.

"You guys looking for Mary and her friend?" he asked from behind the bar.

"Yeah," Cork said, "are they here yet?"

"*Sí*, out back on the patio, with José Muñiz and Hank."

"Mary's a piece of ass, isn't she Johnny?" Cork garbled stonily. Johnny leaned in close to reply.

"She is a very capable *chica, mi amigo. Doctora Maria* can handle the waves and herself very well – *pero Señor Corcho*! Can you handle her!?" We all had a good belly laugh. Cork downed his smoky brown *Barrilito* rum. I dutifully knocked back what was left of my *Don Q Limón*. Cork went straight to the outdoor patio. But I didn't want to meet Monica, so I stayed at the bar.

*

Back by the pool table I watched two *chicas* dance with each other to the *merengue* tunes booming out of the juke box. One of the *chicas* was a beautiful black-haired lesbian in her 40s named Rosa, the other was known locally as

"Anna California," a young blonde in her mid-20's. Anna had been in Rincón only two or three years and already had two children with a local guy named Rodolfo, who beat her emotionally and threatened her physically. She finally forced him out of the house and he threatened to kill any man who tried to date her. Anna was very beautiful, and the nightmare of Rodolfo toughened her up. She did not prefer to be a lesbian, but she was having fun dancing and flirting. She felt free. Anna and Rosa rubbed their breasts and hips together, and the customers smiled, watching closely. People were having a good time.

Meanwhile, two *gringo* automotive workers from Ohio were playing a game of billiards with two Puerto Rican guys on the green felt-topped pool table in the back. Puerto Rican 8-ball is a very difficult game, designed to get players so drunk that their skills are impaired and then it tests their ability under the pressure of the alcohol intake; for billiards requires exquisite eye-hand coordination and great accuracy. At the end of a game of Puerto Rican 8-ball a player cannot sink the eight ball in just any old pocket in order to win. The winner must drop the eight ball in the exact same pocket where he sank his previous and last ball, and only that pocket. Because of this strategic difficulty at the end of the game, the drinking and laughing continues while the players chase the eight ball around the table, hoping for a viable shot. It is very difficult to finish the game when the eight ball is buried in a mess of your opponent's balls, or if your opponent has detained the cue ball in an impossible shot position. Inevitably, much time passes, and while waiting patiently for the final denouement of the game the players feel compelled to order more drinks for each other, as it is considered impolite not to. Therefore, to be good at Puerto Rican 8-ball one must be a steady-handed drunk.

Out on the patio Cork greeted Mary with a peck on the cheek. She gave him a chilly reception. Cork pretended not to notice, greeted everyone at the table, and took a seat between Mary and José Muñiz, a well-known local surfer and surfboard shaper who had been hired to judge the professional surfing competition coming to town.

"José, what do you think of the Corona Pro contest this weekend?" Cork asked him.

"There's a badass swell coming," Muñiz parried.

"They say the contest will have to move over to Juanita's."

"*Claro*! It's gonna sweep around the point from one end to the other," Muñiz replied, "we will have to take it to Juanita's."

Hank Rosenthal didn't want to acknowledge Cork in any way, shape, or form, so he put his face into a pout and did a fake stare off to the side. It was true that he had a crush on Yvonne. He was also jealous that Cork could be with the stunningly sexy Mary North and at the same time conduct a secret affair with the equally attractive Yvonne Acevedo. It didn't sit well with him. Cork carried himself with the unmistakable swagger of a former athlete, a successful New York writer, a man with raw, unapologetic masculinity. Cork could have many women if he wanted to, but this was not an option for Hank, and he had never had an affair before. He and Rachel had been married twenty-one years, raising two unspectacular spoiled children. Great wealth had been transmitted to him when his family sold their pharmaceutical manufacturing business in Rahway, N.J. to Merck. After obtaining a controlling interest in surfing's most prominent website, Hank started a blog to position himself as a senior *kahuna* in the U.S. surfing community; a high net donor writing big checks for worthy causes. Suddenly he was in demand at elite dinners, watermen balls, and *shishi* environmental gigs on both coasts, hobnobbing with pro surfers, industry commissars, and Hollywood producers.

Hank and Rachel sold their split-level in Colonia, New Jersey, bought a gorgeous Victorian pile in Ditmas Park, Brooklyn, a handsome beach house in Montauk, and a Spanish-style retreat in the Rincón hills. Still, basic somatic questions gnawed at Hank's soul. It was an existential crisis; the kind a good rabbi can talk you out of. He was tortured by troublesome questions like, were

there experiences outside the boundaries of middle-class Jewish culture that he would never have access to? Would he ever have sex with another woman before disappearing into death's void? He could see that the gentile surfers all around him were a different breed; irresponsible, crazy, drunk. Most of them kept their marriages together, but many did not. Hank's normative *modus operandi* was to maintain a bit of separation from them, surfing with them during the day, but keeping a safe distance at night. Now he thought maybe there was something to Mikey Surf's takedown of him at Jimmy's Rum Shack. Maybe he *should* hang out and drink and smoke pot with them. Maybe their craziness had some advantages he was not entirely aware of.

When Cork leaned in to peck Mary North on the cheek and Mary turned away with a chilly frown Hank took it as a sign that the rumors about them were true. I was at the bar sipping a chardonnay with Johnny G. when Yvonne Aceve-do strolled in wearing flip-flops and a pair of skimpy shorts revealing pleasantly sexy caramel thighs. She had on a thin top that left her shoulders bare and revealed a nice curve of breast. Yvonne came to the table and greeted everyone. Cork froze up in half-drunk sobriety while Hank faked a cheery know-nothing greeting and turned his back on Yvonne to *faux*-engage with Rachel, who looked right past him to evaluate the competition. She mused to herself, "how could anyone *not* want to sleep with Yvonne Acevedo?"

Cork looked over to the bar and gestured to me to join them. I shifted my posture slightly, pretending not to notice. I was tired of Cork's women problems, and sick of the inevitable competition between Cork and Hank. If Hank would just stop bragging about his dinners in L.A. with Nell Newman, Yvon Chouinard, and Tom Hanks, et al., he might be a pleasant person to have a conversation with. But he never stopped. I was getting ready to leave when Mary walked over to the bar and asked me why I was sitting alone.

"Oh, just quiet time without bullshit," I responded truthfully.

"Yeah, it's hard to be around Cork and Hank. They never stop compet-ing. Come join us, I'll introduce you to Monica." I thanked her, but said I was going, and asked her about the fellowship Cork said she was taking at the University of Pennsylvania medical school.

"Yep. It's a grant for E.R. docs. A research and teaching year will be really good for my career, and Penn's a great school. It's a big change from Puerto Rico, but I'm ready for it."

"Sounds great, congratulations Mary." I got up to go. "Maybe I'll see you guys later." Our eyes met and locked. I always liked her, but always kept a safe distance, pretending to ignore the spark of interest we had in each other. I paid Johnny G, left him a good tip, and walked out past the pool table towards the open doorway that exited into the parking lot, and disappeared between the cars and pick-up trucks under the broad canopy of stars.

I walked home down the dirt and gravel path between cow pastures. When I got to my place I started up my truck and drove over to Calypso bar, a mile or so down beach. There were no cars on the road. A couple of tourists hovered around the bar, but nobody I knew. I got out of the truck to check out the lines of silvery foam peeling into the beach under the moonlight. I could see there would be some type of small rideable surf in the morning, and drove back home. Mary's Suburu wagon was parked in my front yard and Cork was leaning on it, drinking a beer, puffing on a cigarette. Mary and Monica stood nearby.

I parked and greeted them. Cork introduced us and I invited them up for a drink and a bowl of weed. Monica thanked me for inviting them in and made some small talk. She had slightly washed-out straw blonde hair and an attractive European looking face, sort of Dutch. Her lips were prim, like a New England schoolmarm, but also cute and pink and very nice to look at. I reminded myself that no matter what happened, I was not having sex with her.

We went up the steps to the back deck and Cork and I set up the women with a pipe, matches, and a few buds of weed. Then we went to the kitchen to make a pitcher of *mojitos*. I chopped mint leaves while Cork mixed sugar water and cut up limes.

"How was it with Yvonne and Mary both there?" I asked him.

"Weird, really weird."

"Lucky for you Mikey Surf didn't show up."

"Lucky for Hank, too."

"Mikey ripped Hank a new asshole today at the Rum Shack, right in front of Rachel."

"Hank's fucking married," Cork said. I just rolled my eyes.

"Brendan, you can totally nail Monica," Cork added, "she broke up with her boyfriend two months ago."

"Yeah like, but that guy's wife didn't die and he doesn't have a problem fucking other women."

"Accentuate the positive, man! It's been two and a half years. Janice is trying to let you go, but you won't let go. Move on. Monica is a dynamite chick, Dude, and she's hot for you. She has a Ph.D. too. You guys can talk about all that Ph.D. bullshit that no one else gives a shit about."

"Cork, leave it alone. You're higher than Mt. Everest. I can deal with my life, okay?" I filled the pitcher with a big pour of *Don Q* rum, sweet water, bubbly Perrier, and ground in fresh mint leaves. We brought out four glasses full of ice, each with a chunk of fresh lime.

Monica smiled. She was happy to be out of New York. A tropical breeze blew through the deck. The ocean whispered over the reef while we laughed and talked. The neighborhood calico I call Baby slid up the steps and stared at us with big jade green eyes. She scurried back down the steps when Mary tried to entice her to come closer.

Dogs barked in the hills. *Coqui* sang from the holywood and *ceiba* trees, and from the broad green leaves of the *plumeria*. They sang from the almond tree in the back yard, calling out for love in the night.

I stole a glance at Monica's smooth legs, her nicely freckled arms, and the pleasing slope of her breasts. Now I did want to go to bed with her. Looking up at the infinity of stars and galaxies I thought to myself, "My E-E is up there, whirling around in the stars, and I am down here thinking about sex. S.W.O.G. How does Cork get me into these situations?" The *mojitos* were extremely delicious. We passed around the pipe with its bowl of pale green marijuana. The quality was very good.

"Are those *birds* singing?" Monica asked.

"Those are *coqui* tree frogs," said Cork. "The males are marking their territory, looking for females to screw."

"Cork, do you have to be so brutal all the time?" Mary declared, exasperated.

"You mean brutally honest, babe?"

"There's a more sophisticated way to talk about such things. Brendan doesn't talk like that, do you Brendan? Why can't you be more sensitive and civilized like Brendan?"

"That's because he's only half Irish, baby," Cork slurred. "I can't help it." Monica looked at me. I looked at her looking at me. Her eyes were pale gray-blue, like a beautiful Dutch woman. Her flimsy beach dress slipped down. I focused on the point end of her nipples. They were very pleasant nipples.

The night sky held a spectacular infinity. Giant inter-stellar Starships journeyed to distant galaxies, exploring planets far beyond our immediate solar system.

"Do you think there are other planets able to support intelligent life, whatever that means," I asked aloud, to no one in particular. Monica responded that there were dozens of such planets, hundreds, even thousands, each with moisture, atmosphere, vegetation, and sunlight able to engender life. But to get to the closest one, she calculated, was a voyage of 50,000 to 70,000 years, on a spaceship that hadn't even been invented yet.

"Yeah, after fucking up this planet we can go colonize Planet B before the sun burns us up into shards of flaming cinder," Mary put in. "Then we can fuck up Planet B too, killing each other over money and fake religious bullshit." It was an awful vision, but apparently quite true.

"You stoned, MacDuff?" Cork queried. "What else are you thinking about Professor Stone Mason?"

"Oh, deer would be nice," I answered. "Deer could inherit the earth. They seem like lovely individuals... I wonder if when we die we just evaporate into tiny energy stars, or non-organic beings, like one of my colleagues at the university thinks. She thinks invisible inorganic beings live among us and control every-thing. I don't know, does nothing really mean nothing? It's all so mysterious, like, what's outside the universe? Is there any outside to it, and how could there be? Maybe it's like the Möbius Strip Olson and Whalen were talking about."

"Jesus, professor," said Cork. "That's motherfucking cool."

"Brendan, put that in your book," Mary said. "I'd love to read it when you're ready to share."

"Sure Mary, you can read it, if I ever finish the damn thing."

"We're staying at Mare's place tonight, Dude," Cork said, as he stood up to go. "Let's go Mare, Brendan the Space Cowboy can drive Monica home after they get to know each other."

"Oh no, that's okay," I said, "I have work in the morning."

"You don't mind driving me back to Mary's, do you Brendan?" Monica purred. Mary stared at me for a one-second moment, then Cork grabbed her arm and they ran down the steps to her Suburu.

"No, I don't mind," I said. But they were already gone.

"I'll get some Perrier and ice," I said to Monica. "We can chill a bit."
I went to the kitchen and poured out two glasses of Perrier with a small wedge of lime in each, and filled the glasses with ice. Then I paused and added a fat shot of *Don Q* rum into each glass. Monica was standing against the balcony balustrade, gazing out at the wine-dark sea.

"You teach French at N.Y.U.?"

"No, Cork doesn't know what he's talking about. I got my Ph.D. at N.Y.U. I teach at Hunter College and the CUNY Graduate Center. What do you teach?"

"English, American lit, Caribbean lit, composition. I'm up for tenure this year."

"You like living here?"

"Yeah, I guess so. I like being out of the U.S., the ex-pat life. I'm working on a book on the poet Philip Whalen. I wrote a screenplay last year, got another one in the works, that sort of thing. Keep busy."

"Your wife died two years ago?"

"Almost three."

"That has to suck. Did you love her?"

"Sure."

"Cancer?"

"What else?"

We stood at the balustrade, looking out at the ocean. I was trying not to get caught looking, but Monica's butt had a nice bump-out, showing excellent shape through her thin cotton dress. I could sense her moving towards me stealthily, and her dress slipped down in front, revealing more bosom. I stared at the nipple points pushing against her flimsy dress. She moved closer.

"You live in Brooklyn?" I asked nervously and took her hand and kissed her on the mouth.

"Weehawken."

We continued to kiss, and her body fit well into my chest and cock. I slotted it between her thighs and pushed in. My tongue rolled and danced inside her mouth and around her tongue. She had a sweet taste. We kissed passionately. I had not kissed like that in a very long time. Her hair was off-blonde, like flaxen yellow straw. Her eyes were ash gray-blue, befitting sex with a stranger. I slipped my hand under her dress and upwards to touch her nipples. She stroked my cock. We made out ferociously and went into the bedroom to lie down. I was totally lit up with wine, rum, and marijuana. It felt good. I had only just met Monica, but it felt good.

I slid my hand down inside her lacey underwear and touched the wet fishy delight of her pussy with my finger. She moaned nicely. I drew my finger to my mouth. She tasted good. We kissed full on the mouth and Monica undid my belt, slid her hand down my shorts, pulled out my cock, and stroked it, fully extended.

"I don't know if I can do this right now," I said.

"You seem ready."

"But then I always lose it. Maybe I need a shrink."

Monica put her arms around my shoulders and drew me close.

"Look, Brendan, you're a great guy, and a very handsome man. I'm here this week, if you want to go out for a drink or dinner, call me. Mary has my number." Then she pulled down my shorts and sucked my cock. It was a huge turn-on. My eyes fell on a photograph of Janice up on the dresser a few feet away. It was the one where she is looking straight through me, sitting under the big almond tree on the beach. S.W.O.G. I went limp.

"I'm sorry, I..."

"Don't worry about it." Monica followed my eyes to the photograph on the dresser top.

"I should have put it away. I didn't think anyone was coming here tonight. I like you, Monica. I'm having a really good time."

"I like you too."

We were stoned, arms and legs entwined in the darkness. Monica was surely a goddess, too. The ocean tide whispered over the reef. She had cute little freckles on her face and shoulders. That's the last thing I remembered before passing out. In the immediate dream I was making love with a pretty woman with freckles and straw yellow hair. I snored. Monica gathered up her things, walked back to the bar, and got a ride to Mary's place.

Monday 23 January, 2012

There must be a good way to live.
                Rabbit Angstrom

Eros and Civilization

9:12 p.m.   I don't remember how it ended last night with Monica. I remember her beach dress, her nipples. I remember kissing her, but not much else. I hope it went well. I hope I did okay. She seemed like a nice person. This morning I made strong French Roast coffee, washed up, and sat on the meditation cushion for fifteen minutes or so, placing the coffee mug on the floor beside me. I did some last minute prep for school and drove to the campus in Mayagüez. The morning class did not go so well, in my view. Mayagüez is the university's science and technology campus, and this morning my students demonstrated little to no interest in Charles Olson's view of history, and even less in Philip Whalen's Zen Buddhist poetics. The Möbius Strip was at least geometry. They got that much. I concluded that the relentless texting, social media, smart phones, and the shallow media/delusional culture had lulled most of these students into an intellectual dope haze. The interminable chatter, the bullshit content, the shiny corporate networks – dope – intellectual heroin. So I asked myself, what's the antidote for an overdose? What's the cultural narcan? There must be a cultural narcan for these students, otherwise there is no history. Reality is a mere spectacle, a video game in the global theater of the absurd, and the colony of Puerto Rico an obscure episode in the television series called the United States of America. This is what advanced (late) finance capitalism is teaching our young people, while pretending to be neutral and non-ideological. It's brilliant propaganda, however history has not ended. Like Olson said, history is personal and individual, "it is ourselves and nothing outside us." Maybe the narcan is Olson, Jameson, Chomsky, Adorno, Ammiel Alcalay, Norman Fischer; people like that, what they teach and write.

*

The afternoon class went better. The students enjoyed the sexual tension of *The Sun Also Rises*, the randy drinking, the pub talk, the terse descriptions of the Basque countryside. They thought Hemingway's character Brett Ashley was like a sexy rock star. Tomás Cabrera added some thoughtful comments about the role of primitive 'nature' in traditional Spanish bullfighting. As usual, I wondered if that was at all related to the notion of the "Romantic sublime." Before leaving campus I stopped in the English Department office to review the 'call for papers' announcement tacked on the bulletin board. I wanted to make sure that my paper on Whalen and Olson adhered to the advertised topic. I read the announcement and winced. Very few people other than a narrow crew of graduate students and a few dozen professors would digest or even care about the academic jargon that rattled itself off so glibly. It went like this:

> According to Bertolt Brecht, the "estrangement effect" can interrupt the common with the unexpected, and make it more comprehensible, exposing language's capacity to simultaneously obscure and reflect inherited significations... offering an avenue into spectrums of local and foreign, central and marginal, legible and illegible, self and other, old and new.

"Fuck it," I thought to myself, "why can't graduate students write with clarity and precision about something that matters?" I turned and went down the stairs to my office, a tiny, dark space in the basement three floors down. It was a sweltering hot day in Mayagüez. Lines of sweat poured down my forehead as I opened the office door, turned on the air conditioner, and checked email. In new emails two or three students requested a meeting to persuade me to give them a higher grade on their final essay on José González's book *Puerto Rico: The Four-Storeyed Country*.[4] However, I don't just give 'A' grades away. A student would have to engage the González book with evidence of comprehensive and original critical thinking and writing. I feel like this is the best thing I can offer science and technology students, because this class is probably the only humanities class they are required to take before graduation.

There was a knock at my office door and pre-med student Marta Colón opened it, peeked around the edge, and came in. I was startled to see that she was wearing a see-through bathrobe and underneath it a very small and revealing bikini, and nothing else. Marta is an attractive young woman with long dark hair and smooth brown skin. Her eyes sparkled brightly on the palette of an intelligent face.

"Hi professor," Marta beamed, "do you have time to see me?"

"Oh sure, Marta, come in. I totally forgot we were going to talk today." As she took a seat alongside my desk I realized she was soaking wet. She apologized, saying that she did not want to be late for our appointment and had rushed to my office after laps in the university's Olympic pool.

I asked her if she wanted me to turn off the air conditioning but she demurred and jumped right into the topic at hand. She had received an 'A' on the final paper, but she wanted to know if it was really that good, and she wanted to talk about her life and career going forward. She was torn between studying medicine and science, or becoming a writer and studying literature, history, culture, etc.

"Your paper is great," I told her. "I'm impressed with your work. You're pre-med, right?"

---

[4] González argues for Puerto Rico's political and cultural independence from the United States, providing a deft ethno-cultural history of the island. It's a 'must read' for anyone who wants to better comprehend Puerto Rico's contemporary cultural and political status.

"Yes, but I'm not always one-hundred per cent sure of that. There seems to be so much more in life I want to try. My father wants me to be a doctor, but I want more in life than just professional medicine. I think I would be a great doctor, maybe women's health, but I want to write poetry, I want to write books about life. What do you think I should do?" I couldn't help it, but my eyes locked on her lips. The words spilled across the ruby frontier of her mouth like mango stars begging for love and attention. Was she flirting with me? Of course not, this is the routine of beautiful young Puerto Rican college students, their role in life's movie. It wasn't like North America, where the rejection of sensuality in everyday life hovers continuously on the social surface, and sexuality itself is discouraged with a careful tension.

"Marta, your González paper is excellent. I think you can major or minor in literature, American or Spanish, or both, and still have a medical career. You have a pretty solid talent for literature. Dr. William Carlos Williams – a guy half Puerto Rican and half North American-English – was a great 20th century poet, a pediatrician. So you should keep writing, even if you go to med school."

"I want to, I really want to," Marta replied. "My father always says I have to become a doctor, like him, but I want to write."

"There's no reason you can't do both. Keep a notebook with you; in the car, in airplanes, on the bus, in your backpack. Write down everything you see and do, every day, or as many days as possible. A lot of really weird and wonderful things happen every day, insights come and we forget most of them. From your notebooks you can base a novel, poems, fiction, essays, whatever you want to do."

"Are you a writer, professor?" She leaned back in the chair alongside my desk and the bathrobe slipped off her legs. I tried hard not to look as she chattered on about a trip across country to visit medical schools, however now her limbs were completely bare right up to her bikini bottoms. She pretended not to notice any of this, and then slid (purposely or unconsciously?) further down in the chair so that now it was not a chair, but a divan couch in my private office.

"Eros and Civilization," I thought to myself silently, "this is crazy. I have to get out of here."

"I want to see San Francisco and Berkeley," Marta was saying, "and I want to apply to U.C.S.F. and Stanford, maybe a school in L.A. That would be so cool, wouldn't it?"

"Keep a 4.0 average, and you'll have a great shot at getting in," I said. Marta moved her right leg up on the side arm of the chair, showing a sliver of skin between her inner thigh and the thin green bikini line way up in her crotch. I felt dizzy.

"The weather's great in California, Marta. You'll survive there better than a school on the east coast," I told her. "Let me know what happens."

I safely conducted her out of my office and drove back to Rincón. In the center of town I stopped to pick up some *pollo, y arroz y habichuelas* at the hole in the wall restaurant across from the police station. Driving home through the main thoroughfare I spotted Felix Maldonado standing on the corner next to the health center. Felix was a man of about 28, who was congenitally arrested at an early stage of intellectual development and emotional maturity. Socially and intellectually Felix was nine or ten years old, harmless and sweet, a cultural actor who took on public roles in the downtown spectacle of Rincón. He would stand in the town square dressed in cartoonish business attire and a cheap tie, feigning impatience with an imaginary ride to the airport, dragging fake carry-on luggage. From watching American TV Maldonado had learned how to imitate important business people fiddling with smartphones, texting, calling their car service or Uber for a ride to work, and he was quite good at it, down to an annoyed corporate facial expression as I drove by him.

Maldonado functioned comfortably within the town's social structure. Instead of putting him in an expensive psych prison, Puerto Rican culture kept him close in the warm folds of community and everyone in Rincón looked out for him. The old *abuelos* and *abuelas* give him little jobs, like helping Yaya and Papi with errands, organizing shopping carts in the grocery store parking lot, or comically pretending to be a policeman directing automobile traffic.

In Rincón, Felix and others like him can be seen on the sidewalks of the *pueblo* attending to their daily jobs. Perhaps adult children like Felix are fundamentally puzzled by the events and structures of contemporary life; perhaps most of us are.

Before long the mayor of Rincón, Don Carlos Olmeda, gave Felix a part-time job in *La Alcaldía* [5] as a security guard just outside his office, where he sat with the mayor's receptionist, clutching a clipboard. The social construction of Felix Maldonado is, in my view, an anthropological artifact that will eventually be discarded in the dustbin of social history –in the dreary, rationalistic acquisition of U.S. statehood – should it ever come about. Puerto Rico would gain filthy *lucre*, but lose the soul of *Boricua* life.

---

[5] City Hall.

B&W
NOTEBOOK 5

Too many gringos.

Mikey Surf

B&W Notebook 5

Tuesday, 24 January 2012

2:00 p.m.   No school today. I'm writing book reviews for the online literary journal *Jacket 2*. Swellinfo.com says there is a glassy swell in the 2 – 3 ft range kicking off at Shampoo Jack's. But Swellinfo.com consistently underestimates wave size in Rincón, so I figure this means the waves are actually in the 3 – 4 ft. range with head-high sets and an occasional 6' foot bomb. I am heading over there soon.

9:58 p.m.   I ended up paddling out just before 3 p.m. and was lucky enough to snag five or six left peelers jacking up over a definitive spot in the reef. There were no rights to speak of. After an hour or so I dried off and walked over to Jimmy's Rum Shack. Jimmy was behind the stick. As usual, he saw me coming and dished up a glass of chardonnay before I even sat down, calling out, "Brendan McGuinness in the house! Brendan McGuinness in the house!" causing the hotel guests and bar customers to turn their heads. Jimmy Bear, as I have said, is not only an immensely entertaining bartender and a raconteur of the first rank, he is a sports aficionado of the highest order; an expert in NFL football, Major League baseball, NBA basketball, and PGA golf. The only sport he does not know well is surfing, which, ironically, is right here in his backyard. Jim Bear can pick the winner of any play-off sporting event, unless a Kansas City team is involved. But if a K.C. team is involved Jimmy Bear's judgment falters, for he loves his Kansas City teams more than anything else in life. It is the only extraneous factor that mars his otherwise flawless football and baseball analyses.

After two glasses of chardonnay with Jimmy I drove to *Barrio Barrero* to pick-up Mikey Surf for dinner. I promised Mikey we would dine at *El Flamboyan* tonight and then go over to Calypso to meet up with Vance Trento, a friend and former pro surfer in town to judge the Corona Pro contest. When I pulled up to Mikey's house he was in the living room with a beer and a cigarette, listening to old Jan & Dean albums. The lyrics catalogue the Southern California surf scene of the early 1960s, hanging ten on little hot dog waves, drag racing on the 101 Freeway.

Road Kill was sloped across Mikey's lap, his black and white head and long ears hanging down to the floor. Mikey got up and got me a beer from the fridge and sat back down, sucking a drag on his cigarette. His face was red as a chili pepper, with a three day grizzle. He was a good longboarder, broad shouldered, with dark red hair clipped short. He darted a fierce look at me.

"Can you believe Yvonne is fucking that cocksucker, your friend Cork?"

"Dude, I had no idea until you told me."

"Fuck them. I'm gonna get drunk tonight."

"Maybe you should give your liver a break."

"Fuck that."

"At least try to drink a lot of water, man."

We drove to the restaurant down the steep hill of *Camino Martillo* lined with Spanish-style houses packed one alongside the other in bright whites, cool browns, and yellows, with pink, purple, and red flowers sticking out from narrow side yards and flower pots. On the way down the hill a man with dark curly hair and a distressed look on his face was walking up hill in bare feet, his head facing down and slightly to the right. He didn't look up as we passed him.

"Do you know Josué?" Mikey asked me.

"No. I offer him a ride now and then, but he always waves me on."
Mikey took a drag on the cigarette, blowing smoke out the open window.

"Josué walks *Puntás* every day, always looking down and to the right, never down and to the left. He lives on *Cuchillo de Piña*."

"He never smiles."

"Oh, he smiles. He just doesn't smile at *gringos* or tourists. If you were born in *Puntás*, and he has known you since birth, he will smile. He only talks to people of the *barrio* who have lived here their whole lives. He doesn't feel the need to know you or me, or anyone else."

"It's an ethno-cultural thing," I said. Mikey gasped.

"Why do you professors have to use such big bullshit words? Why can't you just say it straight-up like me, without the bullshit?"

"I don't know, Mikey. I guess because we're academics, we talk in codes."

*

The kitchen at *El Flamboyan* was the size of a walk-in closet and the owner, Señor Roberto Méndez, prepared every dish by himself, one plate at a time. His

nephew Papi Soto tried to help his Uncle Roberto in the kitchen by slicing *filetes* of fish and running plates of food out to the tables, but Roberto would not let Papi do any other tasks. Roberto insisted on doing everything else by himself, making one plate of food at a time. Even if fifty people in the dining room were waiting for dinner, Roberto only made one dish at a time, so customers could wait a very long time for their food.

A few weeks earlier a North American *gringa* reviewed *El Flamboyan* in a big online food magazine, informing the world that Chef Roberto Méndez' place was *tranquilo*, that it sat on a hill overlooking the ocean, that it was surrounded by *flamboyan* trees with gorgeous red flowers, and that Chef Roberto served fresh fish caught daily by local fishermen. Further, gushed the review, *El Flamboyan* was an authentic Puerto Rican restaurant that had not yet been discovered. So now it was packed with dozens of *Norteamericano* tourists on vacation. They discovered this authentic restaurant the same way that Cristobol Colón "discovered" Puerto Rico.

Señor Méndez made a big fuss over Mikey when we came in the door, for Mikey and Roberto were very close. "Still didn't get us a table," Mikey quipped, as we ordered drinks from Lorenza the bartender and took our places at the little counter with the local *borrachos*. An hour and a quarter later our Red Snapper *en salsa de ajo* arrived with plantains, *ensalada*, soft white Puerto Rican bread, and *arroz y habichuelas*. It was delicious, for the best price in town. We relaxed and drank with the *borrachos*, who were treated like royalty by Señor Méndez. He had tacked up a makeshift sign on the wall reading, "*Mis borrachos son gente muy fino!*"[6]

I looked around the dining room. North Americans are a very big people – and there are a lot of them — barrel-chested men, large-boned women, numerous children. Hundreds of years of eating cows and potatoes. Mikey had three or four rum *mojitos* with dinner. I had a few glasses of ice-cold wine. When we got up to go. Señor Roberto Méndez came out of his tiny kitchen to see us off.

"You never come here anymore," he said to Mikey.

"Too many gringos."

"So come at lunch," Méndez countered. "It is quiet. We will drink *Gran Añejo* and talk about the old days." Mikey dispensed one of his rare gap-toothed grins to Señor Méndez and we left for Calypso.

The moon poured light on the hills and no car passed us on the road. The transmission slipped out of gear with a whirr and a whine, and I slid it into neutral, and then back into drive, and it caught, so we continued, and parked, and went into the Calypso bar. Puerto Ricans and Americans were drinking and talking under the beat and thrum of *jíbaro* music played by a three-person combo with a *cuatro* guitar, a *güiro* scraper, and a pair of tall bongo drums. Vance Trento sat in the back near the ocean. Mikey went straight for Trento's table, but I stopped at the bar to say hello to Janisa, the bartender. Trento and his wife were sharing a pitcher of rum punch with Cal Ritchie, Cal's wife Carol, and José

---

[6] "My drunks are very fine people!"

Muñiz. Cal was a local waterman known for riding fearsomely large waves with a nonchalance that one percent or perhaps one-half percent of surfers could match. The prior winter he had been photographed by Steve Fitzpatrick streaking across a 40 to 50 foot wave at *Tres Palmas* on a small tow-in board. *Surfer's Journal* published it in the spring issue.

Vance, Cal, and José had hired on as judges for the *Cerveza Corona Pro* contest this coming weekend, a competition conducted by the *Asociación Profesional de Surfing de Puerto Rico*, and I had a media pass so I could interview the contest managers, judges, and competitors for a book, or an article in *The Inertia*. Weather reports indicated that a solid swell was on the way, and pro surfers were arriving in town to assess the local conditions. A category 3 blizzard was on track from Chicago to New York, where it would roll into the North Atlantic and rotate into a giant nor'easter. A second storm with highly turbulent winds was simultaneously slamming its way through the southeastern states. The converging storms were supposed to combine in the Atlantic Ocean off Cape Hatteras sometime on Wednesday. When they collided with the high pressure of the south, the differential would generate strong winds over a vast stretch of ocean, generating a monster swell that would roll south for two or three days before hitting Puerto Rico, whose major surf breaks face the North Atlantic without obstruction. And then there is the Puerto Rico Trench, five hundred miles long and 28,000 feet deep, firing up ocean swells with additional velocity as they roll towards the surfing beaches onshore.

After stopping to chat with Janisa, I made my way over to the table where Mikey was sitting with Vance and Donna Trento and the others. Trento was a competitive surfer back in the day in Jersey, a member of the Dewey Weber World Team. He was a wiry little athlete, extremely effective on almost any type of wave. He tried to introduce me around the table even though I lived in Rincón, and he was essentially a tourist.

"Hey José, Cal, Carol," Trento asked the table, "this is Brendan, do you guys know Brendan McGuinness?"

"*Sí,* the longboard professor, *que tu hace, amigo*? José said.

"Hey Vance, I live here, you don't have to introduce me," I said gamely. "You're the tourist."

"Hey easy on V.T.," Mikey Surf jumped in, "he's classic, you're just a longboard kook." Everyone laughed heartily and Donna Trento managed a thin smile at the corners of her mouth. She was someone who treated a smile as a gift never to be bestowed.

"How are you tonight sweetie?" Carol asked me.

"Doing great, thanks Carol. José, are you and Cal ready for the contest?"

"*Oh sí, vamo'pa'llá*," said José. "It's gonna be one helluva *competencia*, Professor, double-whammy. Two fuggin' storms off Hatteras. They're gonna roll south, Dude! Boom! It's gonna be a gnarly swell."

The waitress brought extra glasses and Cal Ritchie poured rum punch for me and Mikey. Everyone in Rincón was excited about the contest and the predictions for epic surf. Rumor had it pro surfers Sunny Garcia and Shane Dorian were in town, and other pros had been spotted at local breaks. The bar at Calypso was filling up fast. All heads turned when Dorian came in with Otto Flores, Sean Penn, and three women. Penn was trying to disguise himself with a funky hat pulled down over his forehead but several people recognized him, including Mikey Surf.

"Look, there's fucking Sean Penn with Shane Dorian," Mikey slurred, looking over at the movie star. Mikey was solid drunk by now. "Fuggin' guy can't act, no talent. Plays same character every movie."

"That's Sean Penn? ¡Coño, mano!" José exclaimed. "Jeff Spicoli, *Fast Times at Ridgemont High*! Holy Shit, my wife loves that dude!"

"Sure as shit, that's him," Mikey said. "Guy can't act."

"Oh come off it Mikey," said Carol. "Don't be so negative. He's a pretty cool dude – I mean, he helped all those people in Haiti after the hurricane."

"I hear he surfs pretty good, too," added Vance.

"Yeah, he can surf. But he can't act," Mikey insisted, downing his rum punch and pouring another. "I heard he didn't even bring a decent board with him to Haiti. The surf went off for like a week and he had to sit on the beach like a kook with his thumb up his ass!"

"How's classes goin' at the *colegio*?" José asked me, trying to change the subject.

"Good kids, we're reading some pretty cool stuff."

"What do you teach again?" Carol queried. "I can't remember."

"American lit, Puerto Rican and Caribbean lit, with the political history thrown in. This semester we're reading the José González book on originary Puerto Rican culture, Bernardo Vega's *Memoirs*; poems by Corretjer, Julia de Burgos; the Nuyoricans, Miguel Piñero, et cetera. We'll check out the F.B.I. assassinations of Puerto Rican patriots, the *independentistas*. I want the kids to get the real straight-up history, not the official state propaganda."

"Okay Brendan, enough with the big words," Mikey interrupted.

"Nobody knows what the fuck you Marxist professors are talking about."

"*Mira*, Mikey!" José interjected. "I know what he's talking about – *imperialismo Americano* – the fuckin' F.B.I. and C.I.A. assassinations of Puerto Rican patriots. You *norteamericanos* have July 4th Independence Day, when's our *Boricua* Independence Day?!"

"I agree José," Mikey replied. *¡De acuerdo!*"

"Wow, that's cool Brendan," Carol added. "I didn't know English professors taught heavy shit like that. We didn't read stuff like that when I was at college in Gainesville." Mikey guzzled his rum and stood up, a wavering drunkard in the night air. The table looked up at him in fear.

"I gotta say sumpin' to Sean Penn," he marbled.

"Mikey don't," Cal said. "Let it go. We don't want a scene."

"I have to, Cal," Mikey said quietly. "He killed Tim Robbins in *Mystic River*. It was a good fuckin' movie, but that was a bonehead fuckin' move. He got the wrong guy."

"Mikey, *eté* – it's just a movie," José Muñiz said. "*No es la vida real.*"

"*Oh sí, es la vida real*," Mikey averred.

"Mikey, celebrities hate when strangers come up to them," Vance Trento declared. Penn was standing with Shane Dorian, Otto Flores, and the three women, waiting for a table to be cleared off. Mikey got up and slid towards them bumping into chairs and tables along the way, a pirate ship struggling to right itself in rough seas. He tapped Penn on the shoulder.

"Hey Sean, Dude! My sister Cassy Bellamy was 2nd assistant director on *Carlito's Way*, remember her? She said you guys hung out some." Penn swung around to face Mikey. He was about Mikey's height and weight, with a thick wave of hair jumping out from under his floppy hat.

"No shit, really? I remember Cassy, man. What's your name?"

"Mike Bellamy," Mikey managed. "Around here they call me Mikey Surf.

I have a bar in town."

"Your sister's a cool chick, man, good to meet you. I'd love to come to your bar." Penn stuck out his hand out and shook Mikey's.

"You guys are from Hermosa Beach, right?" Penn asked.

"Right on brah," Mikey said. "I learned to surf at the pier when I was a young grom."

"Far fuckin' out. My parents used to drop me off at Bay Street. That was my little kook spot," Penn said.

Mikey was half-wasted but Sean Penn was totally cool about it. He treated Mikey with dignity. I was glad for that because Mikey was under a lot of stress. He had lost two people very close to him in a short span of time, his wife and my wife, Yvonne and Janice. He was coming apart at the seams, drinking like a fish, depressed. The conversation with Penn buoyed him. He felt like the culture at large had endorsed him, and that's all he ever wanted. I could see him smiling broadly as he walked back to the table to sit with us again.

"Sean Penn is so cool," Mikey said. "He was surfing Bay Street in Santa Monica like a little kook while I was down at the pier hangin' ten on my old Dave Sweet. My sister Cassy worked with him on *Carlito's Way*. He played that coke-head lawyer. Fuckin' great actor!"

Wednesday

I talked to Mikey the next day, but he didn't feel too well, waking up on the back deck with a hangover of alcohol poisoning. He didn't relish the thought of being around alcohol, but when he woke up it was already twenty minutes before 11:00 a.m., and the doors of *La Casa Vieja* had to open for lunch so he pulled himself together and got up off the couch. In the bathroom mirror he saw that his eyes were red with dark circles down to his cheeks, so he threw cold water on his face and went into the kitchen to make coffee. Road Kill, stretched out on the floor near the dining table, wagged his tail, happy to see his boss. Mikey turned

on the gas flame under a metal teapot, went to the phone, and speed-dialed Tito, his bar manager.

"*Hola.*"

"*Hola Tito, es Mikey, buen día.*"

"*Lo sé Mikey*, how are you feeling?"

"Not good."

"*Te creo...* I heard you were at Calypso with José Muñiz and Cal Ritchie.

"*Sí...*"

"Sean Penn came in with Otto Flores and some hot *chicas*?"

"*Sí... I got fucked up.*" Tito, can you open the bar. I'm goin' slow here."

"*No problema Mikey*, I go to the bar now."

"*Bueno, gracias, hermano.*" Mikey hung up, dropped a coffee filter into a conical dripper, and poured black coffee grounds into it. He took two aspirin, showered, and dressed for work. He could feel his heart muscle pounding under his *Casa Vieja* tee shirt with the logo of a partly toothless man grinning with a tinge of red beard, a cocktail in one hand, and a surfboard in the other. He slipped on leather sandals. He would be on his feet all day, hung-over, and he would have to make it until five o'clock before permitting himself the drink that would smooth out the jagged edges.

Thurs. morning 26 January

> The so-called 'advanced' countries today offer
> the spectacle of a world from which nature as such
> has been eliminated.
>
> Fredric Jameson

Sometime during last night the two storm systems collided over the Atlantic Ocean off Hatteras, North Carolina, aiming massive waves at the Caribbean. The combined swell had two distinct oceanographic structures. Conditions for the *Cerveza Corona Pro* would not be uniform or unidirectional. The swell was a beast converging on Rincón, and the first heat was Saturday morning. I thought there might be a chance that the contest would have to be cancelled so I telephoned Contest Director Bernhard Vega. He said he was making adjustments to the contest plan. First of all, for the safety of the competitors, two additional lifeguards and four jet skis with highly skilled captains would be needed to pluck surfers from the impact zone and take them out to the lineup for their heats.

Without the jet skis the paddle-outs would be virtually impossible, or would take thirty to forty-five minutes or longer, chewing up the contest clock. The ocean was going to be so rough – the impact zone so impenetrable – that only the most skilled and fearless jet ski operator would be capable of doing this job. Just to be able to see over the crests of the incoming waves and calculate whether it was possible to navigate between them to the outside without getting annihilated, would be an ultimate test of skill and bravery.

Director Vega was confronted with other problems, as well. There would not be enough time for the jet skis to continually run into the beach to re-fuel so there needed to be a second refueling station at sea, just beyond the breakers, to save important chunks of time on the clock.

Secondly, the judging platform Vega typically utilized was not going to be high enough to see over the incoming wave surge, the pounding surf would block their view. The judges, photographers, and assorted personnel managing the event needed to be able to see into the lineup to identify competitors, score rides, and ensure safety. With waves like this, and a lack of reliable channels, it was critical to spot surfers in the impact zone, get to them quickly, and ferry them back out to the lineup while the heat clock was ticking. A drowning or injury would abbreviate the contest, bring negative publicity on Corona, and discredit the viability and judgment of the *Asociación de Surfing Profesional de Puerto Rico*. Vega had 24-hours to solve these operational issues.

Friday 23 January

Playa Juanita   The excitement in Rincón was palpable as tourists and surfers poured into town, flooding the hotels and guesthouses, jamming the bars and cafés. *Cerveza Corona* banners, Puerto Rican and Rincón flags, surfing product logos, and assorted contest graphics fluttered up and down the narrow streets leading into Calypso and Juanita's Beach. *Policía municipal y estatal* directed traffic while Corona refrigerator trucks unloaded hundreds of cases of beer and the volunteers and employees of the *Asociación de Surfing Profesional de Puerto Rico* scurried about setting up marketing paraphernalia, advertising banners, tents, communications gear, food courts, and temporary housing and office structures.

On the narrow strip of beach at *Playa Juanita* and in the scrubby woods alongside tourists marked out their campsites and viewing positions with beach chairs, coolers, blankets, tents, and lean-to's. A large encampment of vintage Volkswagen Campers and Westfalia's from the 1960s and 70s rolled in, setting up gas and charcoal grills, mini-refrigerators, longboards, hammocks, disc players, audio speakers, and little tents for their kids.

*

By 3 p.m. I was back home doing *zazen* with a cup of tea on the floor beside me. It felt good to straighten out the spine and fold my hands in my lap in the cosmic *mudra*. My mind wandered and drifted, but it was pleasant and quiet. I listened to the birds in the trees and tried to imagine what they were saying to one another. I imagined that they were talking to each other about food, other birds, iguanas, the local cats, and the sleeping arrangements for later this evening. Cork came upstairs and looked in through the screen door.

"Dude, sorry to interrupt," Cork said. "We want to have a barbecue here tonight, okay?"

"Sure, what's up?"

"There's so many tourists in town there's nowhere to park. Hank and Iwere thinking everyone could come here tonight and eat and drink, then we'll walk up to the party at Calypso… then in the morning people can park here and we'll walk up the beach for the contest."

"Sounds good. But in the morning I'll probably go to the contest early with José. I have a media pass to the judges' platform."

"You're going to write about it?"

"Yeah, I might. We'll see how it goes."

"Cool. Okay, so me and Rosenthal are coming back here in an hour or so with a shitload of food, water, beer, wine, rum, soda, and we'll do the set-up. You don't have to do anything. Just be a nice host, we'll do the rest."

"You and Rosenthal, huh?"

"Yeah. I'm going to make him pull out his credit card."

"Let's do it."

"I'll call everybody. You invite Mikey and Tito to bartend. We'll put up that tent in the back yard. People are going to crash."

*

The narrow roads into *Punta Higuero* were clogged for miles in every direction with people driving in from all over the island. Hundreds of cars and trucks were parked in the *pueblo*. They hiked past my house to *Playa Juanita* carrying tents, water, food, and gear. The local equestrian club clip-clopped down *Ruta 413* on *Paso Fino* horses with their sharp four-beat sidestep gait. The horses were proud and beautiful, perfectly groomed. They marched in formation to the pasture at the end of Calypso lane, which had been prepared with long troughs of food and water.

La Bomba players came from Mayagüez to the Rincón town square and off-loaded their instruments, costumes, and coolers of beer and rum into old style wooden ox carts. They loaded the carts with big *barrile* drums and the smaller *buleador* and *repicador* drums played with *cuá* sticks and *maracas*, and beaming children were scattered in among the musical cargo. Old men herded the ox carts up *Ruta 413* with rods cut from sea oak. The oxen were massive, bulging with muscle and thick body mass. They were cultural artifacts, strangely out of time, staring about with big hominid eyes.

La Bomba troupe set up for their performance in the roadway outside Calypso, and dozens of *Bomba* aficionados planted their chairs in the front rows of the makeshift stage. Earlier, Cork and Hank had helped me set-up a large tent in the back yard, along with additional shade tarps, umbrellas, three charcoal grills, tubs of ice and ice chests for beer, food, wine, rum, juice, and water, and a long table for the bar. The plan was to grill fish and chicken, have a few drinks, and then walk up the beach to the party at Calypso.

A little after 5 o'clock Mikey Surf and Tito Martinez arrived with a dozen ice-cold bottles of *Don Q Ron de Limón*, bubbly soda, limes, a batch of fresh mint leaves, whole pineapples, and pure organic pineapple juice. Behind them Shampoo Jack and Sophie came with Isabela, Luciano, and two friends. The kids took boogie boards to the little sand spit behind the house and played in the waves. Mikey and Tito made pitchers of *mojitos* and the adults took turns keeping an eye on the kids.

Shampoo passed around a pipe of sweet-smelling mountain herb from the central *cordillera*. Cork O'Reilly and Mary North suddenly appeared in the yard. Shampoo filled the pipe and passed it around again while Mikey and Tito made more *mojitos* for everyone. The grills were afire with wood charcoal, and the chicken and red snapper *filetes* were marinated and dredged in butter, olive oil, chardonnay, lemon, lime, garlic, salt, pepper, and local *salsa picante*. The chefs placed the fish and chicken on the grills and put out big bowls of *arroz y habichuelas*, Puerto Rican *pan con ajo*, and salad.

I wanted to talk to Monica but she kept moving away from me. When I finally cornered her standing alone a few feet from the bar she wasn't that interested in talking.

"Hey Monica," I said. "That was nice last night, thanks for hanging out."

"Oh, thank you Brendan. I feel so much for you and Janice. It's nice that you're still together in spirit." She sidestepped away and went to the back fence. I drifted around the yard and caught a glimpse of Yvonne parking her car out front, so I walked over to greet her, thinking she might be nervous about seeing Mary because of the secret lover's weekend she spent with Cork in New York. Yvonne got out of her car and went straight to the kitchenette door to enlist Rory and his new boyfriend Fabio to go with her to the back yard and shield her from any unpleasantness. Rory had a diplomatic way with people and Fabio was a big muscular guy, so she felt well protected. They invited me into the kitchenette for shots of *chichaito* anise rum, but I demurred and went back to the party.

After a few minutes Yvonne, Rory, and Fabio came and got on line at the bar where Mikey and Tito were working. Mikey turned his back on them, pretending not to notice, and Mary came to the line and stood right behind Yvonne without announcing herself.

"Tito, can we have three *mojitos*?" Yvonne inquired.

"Sure Yvonne, hi fellas. How was New York, Yvonne?" Tito needled her, spotting Mary.

"Oh, someone told you I was in New York?"

"No, I just figured 'cause I didn't see you around for a while. Your family's in Brooklyn, right?"

"Yeah, my mother and brother live by the BQE, you know, South First near Hooper. They live on the block with the *colmado*. My brother has a *gomera* on that block."

"That's chill, my *mamita* lived over by Broadway her whole life. You want *Don Q Cristal* or *Limón*?"

"*Cristal. Házme uno doble.*"

"Your brother still has the *gomera* over there?"

"*Sí, claro*. And I have some paintings in the new art gallery on the corner. It's pretty cool, *una cooperativa socialista*. Nice people." When Yvonne turned around with her drink in hand Mary was right in her face with a fake smile.

"Hi Yvonne, I love your necklace."

"Oh thank you, Mary. You look so beautiful, I'm jealous," Yvonne said, darting away and pulling Rory and Fabio to a group gathered around Cork. He was bragging about his latest novel, while back at the bar Mary did couples research.

"Wow, that was an interesting conversation," she declared to Mikey and Tito. "Yvonne had a weekend trip to New York, huh? That's funny, I could have sworn Cork was in New York at the same time. Gee, what a coincidence!"

"Mary, Yvonne and I are not a couple, so I don't know where she goes or who she fucks," Mikey said, without turning around.

"But you still live together, right?"

"Really, Mary? You're interviewing me?"

"Just a friendly question, Mikey."

"Friendly? I barely know you. You never come to my bar. Come to my bar if you want to talk. We can have a drink."

"*Bueno*," Tito declared with a half-grunt, half-laugh, "we know all the fun shit in this town."

"Okay," Mary said. "I'll take you up on that." She walked over to me with her drink. "Brendan, you know falling asleep on the job is not what girls go for, right? You could at least stay awake." I was off balance, as I hadn't yet cognized the complete memory node of last night with Monica. I knew that we had sexual relations, and I remembered her freckles and straw yellow hair, but what else happened, what it meant, and how it ended, was still quite fuzzy. Mary was insinuating that I fell asleep during sex. And why did women have to tell each other *everything*? Was there no fucking sacred private space?

"You guys should have taken Monica home with you," I replied. "I fell asleep? Great. I didn't even want it to go there. You guys forced her on me." Mary fingered her *mojito*, swishing the lime and mint leaves in the glass with her long red nail-polished finger.

"You can thank your friend Cork for that," Mary retorted. "He thinks he's an expert on love."

"Like a Catholic priest?" I asked.

"*Exacto*, a Catholic priest who racks up mortal sins day in and day out."

"And you believe him?"

"I believe everybody." My eyes fixated for a moment on the sweet shape of Mary's lips, her delicate cupid's bow, and the sexy little blonde hairs on the flesh above the vermilion border.

"By the way, I wouldn't have let you fall asleep," she said, and turned and went to the circle of people gathered around Cork, standing close to Yvonne.

"*Hola* Yvonne," Mary whispered in Yvonne's ear. Yvonne blanched and took a slug of her *mojito*.

"Mary, are you in the contest tomorrow?" Yvonne inquired.

"Umm no, I'm thirty-three and a longboarder. Those waves are going to kill someone, and it's not going to be me." Yvonne prayed that Mary didn't know about her and Cork; their recent love trek to New York.

"Yvonne, come here a second," Mary said, pulling Yvonne aside.

"If you want to go out with Cork, I'm fine with that."

"Why would I want to go out with Cork? What are you talking about?"

"People are saying that you and Cork were in New York together and had, you know, sexual relations."

"They are?"

"Look Yvonne, just do me one favor, if you are fucking him let me know so I can stop sucking his dick. I don't want your pussy juice in my mouth. *¿Entiendes?* And she walked away.

*

Hank and Rachel Rosenthal pulled in the driveway in their shiny German SUV just as José and Dolores Muñiz arrived in their little red Toyota pick-up. The grills in the back yard were smoking with chicken and red snapper. People were lining up to eat and drink. Shampoo passed around a pipe of weed. The island air tasted good in the mouth, the afternoon sun felt good on the face, and for one stoner minute nothing else mattered.

Monica walked across the yard from the back fence to the bar. Hank and Rachel were getting drinks from Mikey while Tito packed beer and wine into the ice chests. Monica waited her turn behind them.

"Hi Mikey," said Rachel, "can I have a *Don Q Limón* on the rocks with a splash of pineapple juice?" Mikey locked his eyes on Rachel's. Her eyes held. Hank was not smiling.

"Sure Rachel, coming up," Mikey said with a devious smile. "What do you want Hank, a glass of milk?" Rachel burst out laughing.

"Oh come on Mikey, you know I don't drink," Hank protested. "Drinking hasn't done you a lot of good." Mikey filled Rachel's glass with rum and ice and left an eighth of an inch at the top for a spot of pineapple juice and a wedge of lime. He poured Hank a glass of juice and gut-perceived that Hank and Rachel were no longer having sex together.

"You know, Hank, it actually has done me a world of good to drink and bartend. It's helped me see through phony, self-promoting jackasses like you, because when you stand behind the bar like this you're the parish priest and therapist combined. You see everything, you hear everything. People tell you their confessions, and you listen and forgive them, or you give them some advice and an ice cold drink. Here's your glass of juicy juice, Hank, is there anything you want to confess?" Hank gave Mikey the middle "fuck you" finger and walked away. Mikey turned to Rachel. "Rachel dear, here's your drink, please enjoy," he said with a big gap-toothed grin.

Monica, standing a couple of feet back, observed the whole exchange.

"Wow *jefe*, you bust the man's *cojones*," Tito chimed in.

"He's got no *cojones*, Tito, that's the point. Young lady what can I get you?" Mikey asked Monica.

"Could I have a glass of white wine?" Tito pulled a bottle of chardonnay out of the ice and handed it up to Mikey.

"Sure. Hi, what's your name?"

"Monica. And you're... ?"

"Mike Bellamy. I haven't seen you around here. Where are you from?"

"New York."

Mikey poured the chardonnay into Monica's glass. She was fascinated that he could be so rude, so macho, right to Hank's face. Tito went up to the kitchen to get more supplies.

"How's the chardonnay?" Mikey inquired.

"It's good. It's very cold."

"So you live in New York?"

"Yeah, Kip's Bay, just off Third Avenue."

"I lived in the East Village, East 7th and B. So who invited you to the party? Are you a friend of Brendan's?"

"No, Mary and Cork invited me. I'm friends with them. What did you do when you lived in New York?"

"Oh, played in a punk rock band, smoked pot, read a lot of books, took classes at C.C.N.Y. and The New School, snorted cocaine. The usual. How did you end up friends with Mary and Cork? He's such an asshole."

"You don't approve of many people do you?"

"I approve of a lot of people, but I have requirements, like basic humility, personal honesty, integrity. Within those guidelines, actually, I'm quite easy on people."

"That gives one hope."

"Cork's an egomaniacal pig. That kind of violates requirement number one. Plus, he's fucking my ex-wife and it's way too soon for that, violation number two." Mikey poured himself a double shot of lemon rum over ice, stirred it with his index finger and threw it back, licking his lips. Monica sipped her wine. She found the conversation intriguing because it was her distinct impression that Mary conceived of her relationship with Cork as monogamous. She appreciated Mikey's ethics.

"Monica, I've got to clean up so we can all go to *La Bomba*," Mikey said. "I own a bar in town, *La Casa Vieja*, two blocks off the square. Stop by after the contest tomorrow. We can have a drink and play some pool. Do you play pool?"

"I can hit the ball."

"That's good enough."

*

The party dispersed from the back yard, and people drifted in couplets and triplets up the beach to Calypso. Rory and Fabio left for San Juan, where they planned to spend the weekend. Tito departed to manage things at *La Casa Vieja*.

I stayed back with Mikey and José Muñiz to clean up and stow the unconsumed food and beverages. Shampoo Jack, Sofia, and Yvonne went up the beach to keep up with the kids scampering in and out of the tide pools. Hank and Rachel followed them a few yards behind with Cork, Mary, Monica, and Dolores. They ambled under the palm trees and sea oaks cantilevered over the beach. On the outer reefs surfers streaked across 10 to 15-ft. waves.

"So you live in New York," Hank queried Monica.

"Yep, I teach at Hunter College and the CUNY Graduate Center."

"Very nice. CUNY. I know Mike Bloomberg," Hank said. "We play squash together sometimes at the Metropolitan Club. He's been good for the city."

"I would prefer someone who cares about public education," Monica quipped. "He lets CUNY starve because it's not a posh school for rich out-of-town yuppies."

"I guess schools divide along class lines, don't they?" Rachel observed.

"Sure do," replied Monica, "maybe we should take Brearley, Dalton, and the rest of the classy private schools and make them public. Then we could take Columbia and N.Y.U. and fold them into CUNY. Single-payer education."

"One big socialist enterprise, huh?" said Hank.

"Food for thought."

*

José, Mikey, and I went out the back gate with a jug of *mojitos* and headed toward Calypso. Just then a round of fireworks went off with a staccato blast and Chinese rockets shot up into the sky signaling the start of the party. The *Bomba* musicians pounded the big *barriles* drums and the *buleadores*, and the dancers came out in flowing *traje* dresses of bright tropical colors. They started the performance with a slave narrative about brutal plantation work conditions, hacking cane in the hot sun, picking coffee beans, bananas, and vegetables, and also about who made love to whom in the vales and ridges of the *cordillera*, and behind the thick trees and underbrush of the coastal plain. American tourists were flashing cameras and smart phones. Cork spotted me, José, and Mikey, and waved us over. We were all together in front of the *La Bomba* stage and Mikey poured fresh *mojitos* for everyone out of the big jug.

> "You know I'm insanely jealous of you," Hank said into Cork's ear.
> "So I've noticed."
> "You have some pretty hot girlfriends."
> "It's a lonely life, Hank. Stick with your wife. She's a keeper."

A keen matriarchal history was apparent in the choreography. The male and female dancers manifested the sore muscles and stiff bones of the back-breaking labor of harvesting sugar cane, but also the simple joys of a day off. When the children were bathed and put to bed the women strutted and swayed, wiggling their butts. They commanded the men to come and dance with them and satisfy their needs, both emotional and physical. The men were shy at first, but soon they smiled broadly with big white teeth and handsome brown skin. They came onto the dance floor with fancy footwork to show they could take care of their women's needs. To the cheers of the crowd they swung around behind their partners and shook and shimmied their thighs into their women's butts in a rhythmic simulation of sex. Then the women came around in front of the men with wide smiles, and the couples bowed.

> "See that," Cork said to Hank. "Women rule the world. Rachel is a goddess."
> "I know," said Hank. "I adore her. It's just tough sometimes being
monogamous, twenty-plus years."
> "Yeah, I guess, I wouldn't know. But I salute you for trying to make it work."
> Five or six *La Bomba* couples came out, one couple at a time, and did
matrimonial rhumbas. Then a female couple came out, did a bow, and performed an erotic dance. They were shy at first, but they responded to the audience's encouragement with verve and enthusiasm. These two women clearly loved each

other. The crowd enjoyed their dignity and free spirit, and their frank and open embrace of sexuality, and gave them a big round of applause.

Then an Afro-Antillean woman jumped onto center stage belting out the lyrics of an ancient slave chant. With her arms and hips rocking and swaying she historicized the perilous voyage on a slaver from West Africa across the Atlantic Ocean's Middle Passage to the Caribbean Sea, reporting how the white masters threw sick and rebellious slaves overboard, killing two-thirds of the human cargo before the ship even landed in the islands. The surviving Africans had incredible pluck, strength, and courage to get across the ocean alive, only to be forced into the debilitating labor of the sugar and coffee plantations. When the dancer was done with her history lesson, she made a deep bow, and the crowd erupted in wild applause.

Out of nowhere Felix Maldonado came jiggling and prancing into the middle of the dance floor dressed up in the comical costume of a traditional *jibaró* peasant with big baggy worker's pants, a peasant's white work shirt, and a green woven palm leaf hat. He held his arms up over his head waving and clapping to the music while the musicians pounded the big *barriles*, shook the *maracas*, and snapped the wooden instruments with their *cuá* sticks. Felix swayed his hips side to side, front to back, in rhythm with the pulsating music. The audience roared its approval as a line of ecstatic children, including Isabela and Luciano and their friends, surged onto the stage in a conga line behind Felix as he led them around the floor and into the packed crowd. Maldonado threaded his way back on stage and the children formed a circle around him. Then he reached into the crowd and pulled Mary North onto the stage while the children cheered him on with screams of delight. Mary gamely danced with Felix, her long, slim frame lightly covered in a beach skirt and a half-top while the children's eyes gleamed with delight shouting "Felix, love her, love her! She is your princess!" "*Felix! Ámala! Ámala! Ella es tu princesa! ¡Ella es tu princesa!*" Fluid and surreal, he twirled Mary around the floor, his eyes fixed on a sliver of moon high in the early evening sky. Then Felix turned and gazed into Mary's eyes, the princess of some heavenly sphere.

"Look at that," Mikey Surf said to José and Dolores, "there is a god after all."

"That man is a saint," said Dolores, "*San Félix de Rincón*."

*

A loud siren cleared the street and a line of *Paso Fino* horses, thirty or forty in all, came prancing through in front of Calypso and people parted to let them pass. Leading the procession was a shiny 1969 red Ford Mustang convertible in mint condition with pure white leather seats. Hoisted over it was a dark blue banner with gold tassels and a *Paso Fino* logo with the words, "*Club Ecuestre de Rincón.*" The *Paso Finos* trotted past in a frisky four-beat strut, capering through the middle of the party. The crowd fell silent in awe of the horses, handsome dark brown ones with shiny manes, pure white ones with yellow hair, jet black stallions, and speckled grays with elegant tails pointed straight up, all prancing down the narrow lane.

Meanwhile inside the bar workers poured dozens of *chichaito* shots of anisette rum and put them on trays for servers who ran them out into the crowd crying, "*¡Chichaito! ¡Chichaito! ¡Vengan, Chichaito para todos!*

Next, a long line of thrumping black and silver Harley motorcycles came roaring through, followed by a procession thirty or forty fully restored Volkswagen bug sedans of all different models and colors from the 1960s and 70s, while *La Bomba* music continued to beat and thrum. The surfing contest air horns blasted and the final procession of the day arrived on foot with *Alcalde Don* Carlos Olmeda, the mayor of Rincón, marching in front with members of the town council, Contest Director Bernhard Vega, and four or five dozen surf competitors, judges, and contest officials. There were twelve surfers across each row walking with their surfboards, men and women with salty blonde, brown, or black hair, tanned, buff, strong, athletic. The front row displayed a banner with a logo of a surfer standing inside a hollow wave, inscribed with the words "*Asociación Profesional de Surfing de Puerto Rico.*" *Alcalde* Carlos Olmeda beamed widely. The whole town was ecstatically happy and everyone consumed the rum *chichaito*. Dolores gave José a full kiss on the mouth, and even Hank Rosenthal knocked back a shot of *cheech* with a big smile.

NOTEBOOK 6

The only possible solace we have in the surf,
especially big surf, is in the fellowship with
the One who created the bitch in the first place.

Tom Curren

Notebook 6, 2012

Saturday, 24 January

5:40 a.m.   I was in a vivid dream before sunrise. The imagery was weird and
ornately detailed. Janice and I were walking around an obscure campus of the
University of Pennsylvania, an ancient Ivy-covered affair tucked away in some
imaginary unexplored part of the Bronx or a remote section of upper Manhattan,
as if something big like a university campus could really be invisible in the Bronx
or Manhattan. It was a weird place for Penn, being out of Philadelphia, so not
many people knew about it, but I knew of it, which was also weird, and now Janice
and I were strolling around the grounds looking for the English Department, or
maybe Charles Bernstein's office, or maybe we were just taking an architecture
tour. The campus was hilly, with wet grass, somber Anglophile architecture, and
trees with autumnal orange, brown, and amber leaves. We held hands and wandered about until we came upon a small stone chapel with an old brass sign out
front that gave a rundown on the origin of the structure. Janice wanted to go
inside, so we did, sitting in the front pew, marveling at the woodwork. Suddenly
the pew shape-shifted and turned into an antique English automobile. I tried to
start the motor, but it hissed and sputtered like the ocean, so I lied down and
tried to sleep in the front seat, but the surf grew louder and louder and pulled me
up almost out of the dream. Janice came into the bedroom with her funny cotton
nightgown on, the old smooth worn-out one with the little blue, red, and yellow
flowers. I felt it brush against me softly as she slid into bed and gently leaned over
and kissed me on the cheek. Her black and silver-streaked ringlets of hair caressed
my forehead. I reached out to touch her thigh. But she was already gone.

The dream was so real, so startling. How does the mind do this with the complete and intricate detail of a movie set?

I got up and looked out the window to the horizon. The sun was about to rise. Maybe the universe is actually a Möbius strip, with no inside or outside. No duality. The sea was indistinguishable from the sky except for big black corduroy lines of surf rolling to shore. The contest would commence in an hour or so.

I started the coffee, turned on my laptop, and went on the Rincón Facebook page. Rumors were flying on the "coconut newswire" that several contestants, both male and female, had withdrawn from the event citing safety reasons. I took a pot of coffee down to Cork and Mary, and two mugs out to the tent where José slept with Dolores. Baby cried for breakfast, staring up at me with big oriental jade eyes. I filled her bowl with dry food and a second dish with a pour of fresh milk, and set out oranges, bananas, and *postres* for breakfast. Soon the

others would arrive and walk down the beach to *Playa Juanita* to watch the first heats of the day. But José and I had to leave for the contest immediately because he was a judge, and I had a media pass and wanted to get there early to record as much detail as possible.

home, 9:08 p.m.   When José and I arrived at the contest site this morning Bernhard Vega and his staff were up on the platform surveying the ocean with binoculars and mugs of hot coffee. Chief Judge Hector Guzmán conferred with fellow judges Iséla Ruiz, Cal Ritchie, and Vance Trento. The waves were in the 8 – 15 foot range. It was a little smaller to the north, but meteorologists were predicting an increase in size during the day. Offshore winds notwithstanding, the dual swell direction was bending the waves into warped contours. A single wave could have two or three distinct sections before exploding on the inside reef. There were many close-outs, a few makeable waves, and occasionally a well-shaped barrel, but the impact zone was a hell-world. It wasn't tough to paddle through, it was impossible to paddle through. There were no channels, and so the functioning of the contest was completely dependent on the jet ski captains. They not only had to ferry contestants out to the lineup for their heats, during the heat they had to locate each surfer who finished a ride in the impact zone, and get that surfer back out to the lineup as soon as possible while the heat clock was ticking.

Through his binoculars Vega spotted the refueling vessel steaming towards *Playa Juanita* from a mile or two south, ensuring the jet skis could refuel at sea as well as on the beach, saving precious minutes. Then Vega spotted a lone surfer battling his way through the shore pound just north of the *Playa Juanita* point. It was the south peak of the break called Dead Man's. Between it and the *Playa Juanita* side was a semi-dry reef that jutted out thirty or forty yards on a left-to-right angle, forming a point break on the *Playa Juanita* side, and a giant left and scary right on the Dead Man's side. Director Vega did not recognize the surfer paddling out as one of his competitors, but he could see that it was a male perhaps between 23 – 28 years old with blonde hair. It was Aidan McClure, hung-over, but an excellent paddler.

"*Mira eso*, dudes," Vega said to his staff, pointing at McClure, who was about to get annihilated by a 14-ft. top-to-bottom barrel that would detonate two or three yards in front of him. The judging platform was mesmerized. But McClure didn't ditch his board and dive deep, he paddled swiftly and directly to the point of impact, did a duck dive under the wave's thick lip, and slid out the other side without much trouble. Now a second, larger and more menacing wave was coming straight for him. The thunder-lip exploded on McClure and he disappeared from view, drilled into the reef like a gnat.

"We may have to send a ski over," Chief Judge Guzmán advised Vega. "This guy could be done. The whole contest could be done."

"Maybe, *pero ¿cómo carajo se va a meter un jet ski a Dead Man's, tan cerca del arrecife? Es suicida.*[7] Let's wait a minute."

After an eternity of ten or eleven seconds McClure popped to the surface, clambered onto his board, and paddled over the next few incoming waves. Then he turned and stroked into a vertical twelve foot elevator shaft. The wave was already throwing over the reef with a long jaggy shoulder, but McClure went anyway. He air-dropped down the face on a right angle with zero traction except for a sliver of inside rail, the tip ends of his quad fins, and a couple of inches of swallowtail at the back end of the board, flying through the first section at airspeed. Then McClure veered straight into the trough and jammed a vertical turn back up to the high line, where he squared out and slotted himself for a gaping throat of barrel pitching over the second ledge. McClure went in the hollow chamber, disappeared from view, and after a three or four second disappearing act came out into daylight. He hit the lip, threw a front-side air, landed it, and zig-zagged a nicely controlled cut-back just a few yards before the sharp teeth of *Juanita's* reef, guiding his board onto the beach. It was a stunning ride, the *de facto* first ride of the contest. But the contest hadn't started yet, and

---

[7] "But how the hell do we send a jet ski into Dead Man's so close to the reef? It's suicidal."

McClure wasn't even signed up.

"Who's that?" Vega asked Cal Ritchie.

"Aidan McClure. He wants a wild card slot."

"Send someone down the beach. If we don't cancel the contest he can have a wild card."

"Okay boss."

*

Hector Guzmán went to the end of the platform to consult with the other judges. Strong rip currents, the bizarre and unpredictable power generated by the compound swell, and the impenetrability of the impact zone were safety concerns. Would the jet ski captains be able to keep up with the safety and rescue issues and still get competitors out to the lineup? Already three men and two women had dropped out of the competition citing risks to their health, and possibly incurring "failure to compete" penalties from the surfing *Asociación*. Talking among themselves, the judges discussed the advantages of a "*force majeure*" decision to cancel the event. A *force majeure* wouldn't penalize any competitor and it would free all parties from liability for economic loss or injury.

"Maybe we should post-pone for a day or two," advised Judge Iséla Ruiz. "But if we do post-pone, we have to call a meeting of the competitors and let them vote on it."

"We do that and the contest goes out of our control," José Muñiz put in, "and then if someone gets hurt the insurance liability is on the *Asociación*, not Corona." Guzmán called for Vega to join them. Bernhard Vega is a tall, athletic man. He bent over them, leaning in to hear their counsel.

"Papi," Chief Judge Guzmán addressed the director, "we think you should go with a *force majeure* decision, because a postponement will throw it open to a group vote, which means chaos and liability. If anyone gets hurt, or worse, the liability for the *Asociación* goes through the roof. Maybe you tell Corona if they want to move forward with this contest, the liability is on them, not the *Asociación Profesional de Surfing*." Vega thought for a moment, then pulled out his cell phone and called Armando Pagán, the Corona marketing director in charge of the contest. Pagán was holed up in a hotel downtown with a young woman named Idélisa, whom he had met during the previous night's festivities. Savagely hung-over, Pagán grabbed his clattering phone off the night table.

"*Hola, Armando Pagán*," he gurgled into the phone, "*Corona Puerto Rico.*"

"*Armando, es Bernhard.*"

"*Acabo de salir de la ducha*,"[8] Armando said, like a drunk pulled over by a cop car, a deer in the headlights.

"Have you seen the surf yet?"

"No, that's your job, *amigo*."

"It's huge, *y muy peligroso.* Five or six entries have dropped out already. My staff want to call it off with a *force majeure* decision. They see an athlete getting hurt, or even worse. A local just got annihilated at Dead Man's. We didn't think he was going to make it." Vega held up his phone to the ocean. Pagán could hear the roar of the waves.

"*Armando, estás allí?*"

"*Sí, estoy pensando.*"[9]

---

[8] "I just got out of the shower."

[9] "Armando, are you there?" "Yea, I was just thinking."

"You sound wasted."

"*No, estoy bien. Sólo pensando.*"

"I have very good people on the jet skis. I have four extra lifeguards. I have refueling offshore. The waves are 'contestable,' but it's really fucking gnarly, *y la responsabilidad de la decisión es Corona*, not the *Asociación*."

"But you are the commissioner and contest director," Armando replied. "Only you can stop a heat or cancel a contest. I have no standing to do that."

"Armando, it's your insurance policy, not the *Asociación*. We can't afford it. We have no money. You have to make the final determination and text it to my phone. I will do whatever you decide."

"Who are the captains on the jet skis?"

"Waldemar Matos, Craig Carson, Cristina Diaz, Leo Richter."

"Okay. *Está bien. Estamos listos entonces.*[10] I'll be down in fifteen minutes."

*

Vega and Guzmán opted to start the contest with a round of women's heats at 7:30 a.m. Because several surfers declined to compete, there were now 22 women and 48 men in the competition. At quarter to seven contest announcer Pito Mendoza got on the main stage microphone to kick-off the 25th annual Corona Pro Surfing Competition.

"*Atención todos, Bienvenidos al 25 anual Corona Extra Pro Surfing Competencia aquí en la Playa Juanita's en Rincón, bajo la dirección de la Asociación Profesional de Surfing de Puerto Rico y nuestros patrocinadores Cerveza Corona Extra y O'Neill Wetsuits y productos de surfing*. We are the only professional circuit in Puerto Rico, a three-star event with a $60,000 purse for each division, and this is the third and final contest of the season.

"I also want to thank our co-sponsors *Claro PR Teléfono, Tequila José Cuervo, WAPA-TV*, and *El Nuevo Día*.

---

[10] "Oh, that's good. We're good to go then."

"En quince minutos vamos a llamar al primer heat para la división femenina, primero quiero presentarme y nuestros jueces...[11] *Hector Guzmán, José Muñiz, Cal Ritchie, Iséla Ruiz, Vance Trento,* y *el* 'contest director' *Bernhard Vega..."*

At that moment Corona marketing director Pagán stumbled onto the stage with Idélisa. Tripping over cables and wires, they nearly demolished a video camera set up on a tripod, dodging equipment and wires until they made it safely to the mic stand and stood next to Vega, beaming broadly.

"Y por favor también la bienvenida a nuestro gran patrocinador Cerveza Corona Puerto Rico y su director de marketing, Armando Pagán!" announcer Pito Mendoza declared. Armando and Idélisa flashed big smiles as the cameras rolled, snapped, and popped, and videographers panned the stage, including Shampoo Jack, who alternatively took stills and captured live-stream video of the surf, the crowd, and the entire spectacle. The audience cheered and jeered and roared their approval of Corona, and Armando and Idélisa waved back like movie stars on the runway. Next Contest Director Vega called for a private pre-contest 'briefing' with the judges, jet ski captains, and other key staff on the main platform. He invited a well known local *kahuna,* Waggy Moreno, to join them as a representative of the Rincón community. Even though most of the staff knew Waggy, or knew of him, some didn't, and so Vega introduced him.

"Judges, safety personnel, jet ski captains, administrative and marketing people, I have asked Waggy Moreno to join us in this briefing. As many of you know, he is a highly respected member of this community, and he has surfed these waves for over forty years. Waggy agrees that the surf conditions today are challenging; but he also agrees that they are contestable. Today here at *Playa Juanita* could be compared to a crazy day at Supertubos, or Ocean Beach, or Biarritz, and they do not cancel. So we do not cancel. Perhaps today, if they gain the points, one of our own Puerto Rican surfers will win the right to represent our island on the World Tour. But that is a matter for the history books, because

---

[11] "In fifteen minutes we will call the first heat for the women's division, but first I want to introduce myself and our judges..."

today all contestants, whether they are from Puerto Rico, Hawaii, Brazil, Florida, California, or wherever, will be scored fairly and objectively and treated equally by our judges. My friends, the impact zone you see is ferocious – there are no channels to speak of. So I need everyone on the tower and the platform to maintain visual contact with their designated surfers at all times, in every heat, and promptly report any emergencies to the safety directors who will have continual radio contact with the jet ski captains. Every surfer must be tracked until they are picked up by Waldy, Cristina, Craig Carson, or Leo, and brought back out to the lineup. Safety is our primary concern, not the length of any particular heat. If a heat has to go longer, it goes longer. Any questions?" There were no questions for Director Vega from the assembled staff and judges.

"Waggy, do you have anything to say?" Vega asked.

"I can only say may the best surfers win!" declared Waggy, "and thank you for your contribution in Rincón! *¡Comience el contest!*"

*

Dolores Muñiz, Cork and Mary, and Hank and Rachel Rosenthal came down the beach to *Playa Juanita* and found a patch of sand and a shade tree twenty or so yards up from the platform. Camera drones whirred overhead shooting photos of the crowd on the beach and spinning out to sea for aerial shots of the riders up on waves. Mikey Surf arrived with Monica.

"What the fuck, Mikey and Monica?" Cork muttered to Mary under his breath.

"It didn't work out with her and Brendan," Mary whispered. "Mikey invited her out for a glass of wine and a game of pool. His honesty impresses her."

"Maybe she could've given Brendan a second chance?"

"Cork, we make our beds and then we sleep in them. Brendan is still stuck on Janice, what do you want Monica to do? And you clearly want to fuck around with Yvonne, so what do you want me to do? I can't take the lies and

deception. I'm going to Philadelphia without you."

The contest air horn honked up and down the beach signaling the ten minute warning for the first heat, and Pito Mendoza shouted through the loud-speakers in Spanish and English for the first set of women competitors to report:

"Surfers Lila Lebrón, Roberta Lima, K.C. Kaminski, Amory Murphy, Jasmila Ventura," Mendoza's voice boomed out through speakers strung in trees and poles up and down *Playa Juanita*, "report to the jet ski captains on the beach in front of the judges' platform!"

Standing on the platform with fellow judge Cal Ritchie, Vance Trento spotted Aidan McClure walking up the beach with his 5'5" swallowtail quad tucked under his arm. Cal didn't think a judge should talk to him off book, so they sent Shampoo Jack down to offer McClure a wild card slot, and not to worry about the $100 entrance fee.

Craig Carson ferried Lila Lebrón out to the lineup. A native of Aguadilla, P.R., Lebrón had completed one season on the world tour, got eliminated in the final event, and was now focused on earning enough points to return to professional surfing's top circuit. She was extremely competitive and nearly fearless, but the surf at *Playa Juanita* this day was not 'normal.' Even on a heavy day at Margaret River, Pipe, Sunset, or Steamer Lane, there were fairly reliable channels for surfers to paddle through. Today at *Playa Juanita* there were no channels, and *Juanita's* is not a beach break, not even close, so the massive volumes of water flowing through the multiple impact zones made the physicality of the contest extremely challenging.

Carson headed straight out with Lebrón and her surfboard strapped to the back end of the personal watercraft. At the inside ledge they were confronted by a huge, impenetrable incoming set so Carson veered the ski sharply to the right and gunned it down the line looking for a makeable channel. A few seconds later he spotted a flat lane around the tail end of a big left, but as he began to jam the jet ski into the lane a big set popped up, and so he bailed and swung back to the inside.

They probed the impact zone, zipping back and forth until at last there was a twenty-second lull and Carson gunned it through small bumps and lumps of

water until they penetrated out to the lineup. Lebrón undid the straps, grabbed her board and dove in. She immediately tried to figure out the best spot to grab an incoming wave and at the same time avoid a 'clean-up' bomb that would take her down in a severe trouncing. Suddenly a set of three decently shaped 13 – 15 foot waves came right to her, so she eyeballed a tree on the beach and fixed her location so she could slot herself in this spot for the heat. Within fifteen or twenty minutes all four women competitors were in the lineup, jostling for position.

In the Puerto Rico competitive circuit this year each contestant in a heat was evaluated on their three best waves. The following year, in order to conform to new World Surf League rules, the competitive format was changed to include only the two best waves per heat. This was the last year of the 3-wave competitive heats. Using a simple scale of 1 – 10, the highest score for a ride is 8 – 10 points for an excellent performance, 6 – 7.9 points for a good performance, 4 – 5.9 for an average ride, 2 – 3.9 for a merely fair ride, and 1 – 1.9 for a very weak ride. There would be no limit to the number of waves a surfer could take during the heat, but only the three highest scores would be added together for each surfer's heat total.

The judges on the platform were ready to go with their score sheets and tabulators, so Contest Director Bernhard Vega signaled the start of the heat with a single loud blast of the air horn. Most of the waves were rights, although now and then a left or a combo A-frame rolled through. Lila Lebrón was furthest over on the main peak jostling with Amory Murphy as an outside set darkened the horizon. The women scrambled for position. The first wave in the set was an impossible close-out, but the second was a fairly well-shaped right with a decent shoulder, probably makeable, with a top to bottom face of about 15 or 16 feet, slightly more than double-overhead. By paddling further and further toward the critical take-off slot Murphy was intentionally pushing Lebrón further and further into a risky take-off position. It was a smart tactical move on Murphy's part and her plan of attack worked. Lebrón paddled a bit too far into the gaping pit of the wave and it nearly sacked her. She had to bail out and duck through the lip without getting sucked over the falls fifteen feet down into the trough, where she would lose extremely valuable minutes.

When Lila Lebrón lost her inside position, Amory Murphy took command of the wave and paddled into it with a few decisive strokes. She careened down the face with a burst of speed, ripped a solid turn off the bottom and streaked across a big fast-breaking section, tucked inside the barrel, hitting the final close-out lip and landing a stylish frontside air. Murphy's ride was scored an 8.1 by the judges, a very good initial score.

K.C. Kaminski from Jersey was unnerved by the size and ferocity of the surf and hung back from the best sets, and Jasmila Ventura's wave selection was her downfall. She went on three consecutive close-outs that offered little potential for decent scoring. Roberta Lima picked off a few smaller waves for decent middling scores, but she wasn't reading the main peak well, and wasn't able to get into any of the more spectacular barrels. Meanwhile, chastened by her tactical error on the first set of the heat, Lebrón aggressively picked off two superbly score-able waves, massive steep right-handers with long tapering shoulders. She racked up an 8.3 and a 7.7, taking the lead from Murphy. After forty-five minutes the heat ended with a double blast on the air horn, leaving Lebrón in front and Murphy in second place. They proceeded to the quarter-final heats the next day.

Meanwhile, the first men's heat was called up at roughly 2 p.m., with the outside bomber sets now in the 15 – 18 ft. range with perhaps an occasional 20-ft. bomb. The impact zone was even more impenetrable and so the contest was now even more dependent on the jet ski captain's ability to taxi competitors out to the lineup and pluck them out of the impact zone when their rides ended.

On day two the wind went side-shore, with a slight offshore angle on the *Playa Juanita* side of the point. The shape of the swell had improved, the wave faces were smoother, and the size and power had increased. By early afternoon Lila Lebrón dominated the final women's heat with two rides in the nine point range, pushing Amory Murphy into second place, and Roberta Lima of Brazil into the 3rd place slot. Lebrón was exhilarated with her now improved chances of getting back on the world tour.

*

Back at the house early evening, Cork and I talked over the day's events with a beer and a taste of *Don Q* rum. Sitting on the deck we spotted the two brothers next door standing in the jumble of animal cages and junk underneath their house. The older brother, perhaps 15 or 16, was tall and thin, a somewhat sullen boy in my estimation. He held a long knife in one hand. They stood together a moment, staring at five plump brown rabbits huddled in two separate cages alongside each other. Typically the roosters screeched and the hens clucked in a non-stop cacophony of animal riot, but the menagerie fell silent as the animals warily eyed the boys. The older boy walked over to the rabbits while his little brother stayed back, clutching a cloth sack. He was 6 or 7 at most. Next the older boy opened one of the cages and grabbed a handsome brown rabbit by the neck as the other animals watched. He held the rabbit up at eye level with its torso perpendicular to the ground as it struggled and squirmed. Then the boy jerked the rabbit's head back sharply, broke its neck with one arm, and slit its throat with the knife. Blood spurted to the dirt floor. There wasn't a peep from the other animals. The chubby white rabbit who shared a cage with the black and orange rooster trembled with fear and turned her back on the scene, unable to countenance the violence. Then the older boy slit the throats of the four remaining rabbits. Their blood poured down to the ground. He set their corpses in a neat mortuary row and signaled for his little brother to bring the cloth sack to him. They placed the rabbits in the sack, one by one. The younger boy showed no emotion, but the rooster, who had not screeched a single locution during the entire episode, squawked a sad series of funereal notes for the dead rabbits. Cork and I watched closely as the boys went up the concrete steps to the outdoor kitchen one level up to dress the meat.

"Always swim up"

Glaucon: Do you think there is a good of the kind we would
choose to have because we value it for its own sake, and not
from any desire for its results? Enjoyment, for example, and
pleasures which are harmless and produce no consequences
for the future beyond enjoyment for the person who possesses them.

Socrates: Yes, I do think there is a good of this kind.

Plato, The Republic

Sure it's a game. But the winners aren't playing for fun.
They're playing for cash, and what that means to surfing
depends on what surfing means to you.

Surfer Magazine

Sunday 25 January

10 p.m.   This morning I let José go down to the contest without me and I
walked the beach by myself in the shade of dawn. Yesterday's men's competition
hardened into a battle royale between two Puerto Ricans, Gabriel Cabrera and
Guillermo Padilla, the Brazilian pro Bino Medina, and New Jersey's Aidan
McClure, who winters in Puerto Rico. These four eliminated several top seeds in
the early rounds, including local champions Barry Roth and Alberto Moreda,
Hawai'ian pro Damien Hopper, and Brazil's Bruno de Souza.

Walking to Juanita's I spotted Cabrera paddling in from Dogman's and we
walked up to the contest together. Gabby told me that his friend Leif Engstrom
paddled out at Dogman's a few minutes before him, and they surfed in the first
hour after the sun peeked over the horizon. Leif is a great surfer, but he had been
eliminated in a very tough heat the day before. Gabby told me he went out at
Dogman's early to get one or two waves to loosen up his sore limbs and muscles,

and ignite the brain cells in his feet, ankles, and tendons for the next heat. He was hoping that a couple of decent rides would drain the hurt from his body, take the lump out of his throat, and eradicate the fear of failure from his mind. For on this day to defeat Padilla, Medina, and McClure, he would have to turn in an unprecedented performance of grace, power, and style. Style counts in surfing as in few other sports. The grace and flow of the ice skater, the display of form and style that separates a great gymnast from a merely good one, is also a huge factor in the sport of surfing. Contest judges may, without guilt or retribution, add points to a surfer's score when the athlete shows uncommon grace and flow, great poise in critically tenuous situations, or an unusually stylish operation of body and mind on a wave, including a tasteful completion in the final seconds of the ride.

As we walked Gabby told me that he did not underestimate the threat from Guillermo Padilla of San Juan. Padilla was known for a relaxed technique in the barrel that suddenly gave way to explosive moves and high-flying airs off the face of the wave. As for Bino Medina, most people who followed professional surfing had already concluded that this young Brazilian lefty was only one contest away from earning a spot on the World Tour. Every pro surfer on the tour who had seen Medina surf in person or on video knew he would soon be competing with them, driving powerful backside turns and airs with his crazy 180° vision that could read a right-hand wave as well or better than any regular-footer.

And then there was Aidan McClure, the black hole, the unknowable unfathomable; not even a pro, the last minute 'wild card' that Vega had let into the contest. McClure was indeed a 'wild' card. After learning to surf in Jersey's summer slop, the occasional epic hurricane swell, and the thick icy barrels of the North Atlantic winter, he spent four years on Oahu's North Shore and three winters in Rincón. In Gabby's reckoning, the problem with McClure was that he was the only surfer in the final heat who knew Juanita's intimately and could read the layout of the several peaks and negotiate them in ten to eighteen foot surf. Plus, McClure was a fearless balls-to-the-wall surfer. When he was on, no one could touch him. Gabby would have to be on his best game.

*

I was up on the platform taking notes when the final men's heat was maybe fifteen or twenty minutes off. McClure was sitting on the beach below with the other three surfers in his heat. I watched as he got up and walked up twenty or thirty yards to where Mikey, Monica, Cork and the others were hanging out. He wanted a beer, just one beer to loosen up his muscles and take the pain away. He asked Mikey for a *Cerveza Medalla* and Mikey dug into his cooler and brought out a can of beer.

"Thanks Mikey," McClure said.

"It's okay man. Just win this thing," Mikey said, "hit that fuckin' ledge and go nuclear, okay big shot?"

McClure took the beer and sauntered up to the parking lot alongside Calypso and got in his Buick *Le Sabre*. The brown-eyed girl was slouched in the passenger seat. They shared the *Medalla* and a cigarette, while his heat mates Cabrera, Padilla, and Medina sat on the beach with their coaches and trainers.

Looking down from the platform and spotting only three of the final heat's contestants, Director Vega was alarmed and recruited José Muñiz and Shampoo Jack to find McClure. Under Puerto Rico contest rules if a surfer misses the call-up for a final heat, their position in the heat transfers to the next ranking competitor, so he could not waste any time, as the heat was about to kick-off. The Corona circuit was the apex of Vega's professional life, requiring professional management on his part. If the wild card maniac Aidan McClure was going to fuck things up, Vega himself would pull the plug on him. Suddenly José Muñiz eyeballed McClure sitting in his *Le Sabre* in the parking lot.

"*Allí está*," Muñiz handed his binoculars to Director Vega. "*En esa mierda de* Buick, *con los* roof racks. *Mira*. He's drinking a *Medalla* in the front seat."

"*Coño mano.* Jack! Vega commanded Shampoo, "get his ass down here. And make sure he's sober!" Shampoo shook off his camera gear and ran down the platform and up the hill to the Buick. McClure was sitting in the driver's seat, sipping the beer, smoking the cigarette. Jack went straight to McClure's side of the car so the girl looked out her window on the passenger side, never looking over at Shampoo.

"Aidan, what the fuck are you doing?" Shampoo barked. "They're calling up your final, man! Vega wants you on the beach now!" McClure passed the cigarette to the girl, who continued gazing out her window.

"You're drinking before your final fucking heat?" Shampoo demanded, "and what is her fucking problem?!"

"Dude! I'm tight and sore all over. If I have one beer, I drop in and the ride is smooth, I'm in control. Chill Jacko, I'm splitting the *Medalla* with her," he said, gesturing to the girl. "I'm not even drinking the whole thing, Dude – and don't worry about her. She doesn't like old men." Shampoo trotted back down the hill followed by McClure with the 5'5" swallowtail quad slung under his arm. Shampoo flashed Vega the 'hang loose' gizmo signal meaning McClure was fit to compete. Vega alerted Chief Judge Guzmán to squawk the 5-minute warning on the air horn.

It was the final heat of the contest, determining the winner of the men's division.

I watched from the platform as Gabby Cabrera and Guillermo Padilla went out on jet skis, and then Bino Medina. Finally, Craig Carson rotated back in and picked up McClure. As the other three contestants waited in the lineup, Carson and McClure raced back and forth in front of the impact zone looking for a way to break through. There were eight and ten wave sets, and they were rolling in with virtually no safe separation between them, but the heat could not start until McClure was positioned in the lineup with the other competitors. Carson gunned the watercraft up and down the impact zone as waves loomed just beyond. Frustrated, Carson drove the ski down to the far north end of the point, just this side of Dead Man's, where the reef was jagged and incoming surf could easily drag a personal water craft and its occupants right over its sharp teeth.

This was a dangerous spot to penetrate out, but standing up in the saddle Craig Carson saw an opportunity, a one wave set, a 16 or 18 foot peak which, if he succeeded in getting over it, would allow them to fire straight out 25 or 30 yards and then swing over to the lineup. He opened up the throttle and gunned it. The lip of the wave was already feathering and threatening to throw down as McClure gripped the passenger safety bars.

"Ready for some shit, Aidan? We might not make it over."

"Go for it, Dude," Aidan said. "Always swim up, that's what they say in Hawai'i, brah. Always swim up."

Up and down *Playa Juanita* hundreds of spectators stood up from their beach chairs mesmerized by Carson's suicidal gamble. Every judge, photographer, and staff person on the platform had their eyes fixed on the spectacle. I could see that the top edge of the wave careening towards Carson and McClure had already begun a Niagara Falls-type pitch to the bottom as they started up its face. My guess was that this enormous wave was going to flip them over the falls backwards in an uncontrollable explosion. The fucking jet ski was no longer a water safety craft but death's anchor around their necks. Carson opened up the throttle to max speed and jammed the ski up the wave and just over the lip with not more than eighth of a second to spare. Any hesitation would have doomed them. A gasp went up from the beach as Carson wiped the spray from his eyes to see two additional critical waves thundering directly at them, both of them as deadly as the first. However, being a few yards further out they made it safely over both.

*

One blast of the air horn kicked off the final heat. The first place win came with a $40,000 purse, $15,000 for second place, and $5,000 for third. As with conditions during the women's division, the unpredictable nature of the swell underscored the importance of each surfer's positioning in the lineup and intelligent wave selection. Cabrera and McClure were locals. They had been in this situation in this spot hundreds of times. They knew in their bones that an incoming set (especially a large one) could swing wide around the point and break further out, putting it out of play for those surfers positioned too far inside and close to first peak. Cabrera's coach, Alberto Alvarez, had given him a mantra to chant to himself: "wave selection, wave selection, wave selection." Alvarez advised Gabby to sometimes let the first and maybe even the second wave of a set pass by (based on his perception of them), because statistically the third or fourth wave of the set is often the best. It is often bigger and better shaped, and when the first two waves drag volumes of water off the bottom reef, it clears the way for a faster and hollower barrel that can enable a higher score.

Three-quarters of the way through the heat Gabby Cabrera was in the lead with a composite two-wave score of 16.8 out of a possible 20, followed by Guillermo Padilla with 14.7, and Bino Medina with a 13.2. McClure had caught only one wave at this point, a 7.4, and he was strategizing for a big ledging pit to project him into a play for first place. McClure spotted a large outside set marching toward them, and Padilla and Medina were too far inside and too close to first peak to have any realistic shot at it. The set was swinging wide. Only McClure and Cabrera were in any position to take advantage of it. They paddle-battled out trying to box each other into a less than desirable position, since under contest rules only the "inside" person closest to the breaking part of the wave has the priority position and the right-of-way. The first wave wasn't even remotely makeable, but the second was a well-shaped 15-17 ft. swell already feathering at the top. With his solid point lead Cabrera had no intention of risking this wave, so he faked a play for it, pushing McClure further and further into the pit. The lip was throwing out when McClure ditched down the face airborne and got buried head to toe in soup. He somehow slipped out the bottom, connected a hairball turn on one rail and one fin, and shot back up into the smoking, spitting core, slotting himself in the barrel and sticking one hand in the wave wall to slow himself down and go deeper inside. The wave slammed into the second ledge. Time stood still. McClure disappeared from view for eighteen or twenty yards. Coming out of the chamber he set his 5'5" quad on the lip and slid across the top edge of the wave in a floater, before landing safely in the trough, and kicking out. The judges pegged it a 9.2, which put him at 16.6, within a hair's breadth of Cabrera's first place 16.8. This meant that Cabrera's and McClure's next and final waves would determine the 1st place winner, because the set was hitting further and further out, and Padilla and Medina were way too far inside to have a shot at any of it.

The heat clock kept ticking as McClure was ferried back out on Cristina Moreno's jet ski. Pito Mendoza broadcasted the current point structure so that each surfer in the heat could know the exact score he needed for victory. Mendoza shouted into the sound system, "In blue jersey, Gabby Cabrera at 16.8," Mendoza declared, "in red jersey Aidan McClure just scored a 9.2 so he is now at 16.6, "in yellow jersey Guillermo Padilla is at 14.7, and in white jersey Bino Medina is at 13.8. Gentlemen, you have one minute and forty seconds left in the final heat!"

Padilla needed one solid, perfect, outstanding ride to put him in potential position for a first or second place showing. He recognized the weakness of his

interior position and started paddling furiously to the outside to try and nail down an incoming wave with a minute and twenty or thirty seconds remaining. However, Bino Medina hesitated for several seconds, got slammed by the incoming set, and was dragged in thirty or forty additional yards, rolling and bobbing in the heavy soup, and thus losing any opportunity to move up to second or third place.

Padilla was digging for the outside when a gnarly set wave came straight at him. He threw himself into it like a *vaquero* facing a murderous bull. The swell jacked-up in a deep jaw over the reef and as he flew down the shaft it rocked and bucked and half-way down, as he was about to set his bottom turn, the wave shook and shimmied and the nose-tip of his board caught a stray blob of water, and Padilla was spun into an airborne free-fall head first into the impact zone, his board flapping and twisting in the wind behind him. Guillermo Padilla was done. There was no time on the heat clock for him to recover and rack up another score. The best he could do was settle for third place.

First and second place in the men's division was now a two-man contest between Gabby Cabrera at 16.8 points and Aidan McClure at 16.6 points. There was enough time on the heat clock for each of them to get one more wave, and that wave would determine the final outcome. Cristina Moreno heard Pito Mendoza's score rundown in her earpiece as she dropped McClure off in the lineup several yards from Cabrera.

"Gabby's at 16.8, you're at 16.6," she shouted over the jet ski motor to McClure. "There's a minute or a minute and fifteen seconds left, Aidan. Good luck!"

"Yeah, Fuck it!" McClure shouted back.

"Fuck it? Fuck what?" Cristina replied, but McClure paddled away without answering.
A decent set in the ten to thirteen foot range was rolling in. Gabby let the first wave pass, and when the second one came straight to him he could see it was a clean, shapely peak and he went for it.

"*Gánalo por tu esposa y tu hijo!*" McClure shouted to Gabby, advising him to win the contest for his wife and newborn son. Gabby caught the wave and escalated to the high line, powering across the steep ridge for twenty or thirty yards before jamming to the bottom and blasting a perpendicular bottom turn straight back up. He got nicely barreled across the second ledge of reef, slid across the lip, and then kicked out for a solid scoring wave. McClure couldn't observe the whole ride from behind, but when he spotted Gabby flying out the far end, he knew Gabby had racked up a good score. Now a thick hollow barrel came straight for McClure, spitting a cloud of spray and smoke out of its tubular chamber. He stroked into it with twenty seconds left on the clock. This wave easily could have elevated McClure into first place, but instead he dropped in with his arms hung limply down his sides to his waist. He performed no rail-edge bottom turn, no effort at radical maneuvers; just skidded straight in without a turn and skimmed ahead of the whitewater soup for fifteen or twenty yards until it caught up with him and he fell prone on the board and rode in flat on his belly, bucking and jerking in the frothy churn. The heat clock expired. McClure had thrown first place to Cabrera. A blast on the horn signaled the end of the men's division finals. McClure finished with a 1-pt. ride, while Gabby's last ride scored an 8.4. The judges' platform was aghast in utter shock, speechless. The crowd on the beach stood up in confusion and consternation as McClure came into the beach.

"¡Coño mano! What the fuck *es eso*?!" Chief Judge Guzmán exclaimed.

"What the *fuuuck*!" cried Judge Iséla Ruiz.

"What the *fuck* is happening?" Cal Ritchie asked Vance Trento, who was standing next to him with binoculars.

"McClure threw it, McClure threw the contest."

"¡*Nunca he visto nada como esto*!" Ruiz added.

"What's happening here, Shampoo?" Director Vega said to Shampoo Jack, "do you know this kid?"

"Looks like he threw it, Bernhard," said Shampoo, "maybe he didn't want first place. Maybe he wanted no place."

"*Jefe*, I'll check the *libro de reglas*," Judge Guzmán said into Vega's ear. "We have to decide if this kid is disqualified, or if he can have second place. Maybe it was unsportsmanlike conduct?" McClure's final score was 17.6 out of a possible 30, while Cabrera did well on his last ride, pushing up his final score to 25.2. The men's event was now in a state of regulatory disarray. By intentionally fucking up his last ride, McClure had surely forfeited first place, and maybe any place in the finals. Shampoo Jack panned his video camera over a disturbance on the beach. A large group of Puerto Rican fans and spectators were gathered around Waggy Moreno, and they were agitated, spoiling for a fight. Their boy Gabby Cabrera didn't have a 'clean' win. He won, but the *gringo* McClure had stained it with his unseemly performance. The mob pressed around Waggy, tempers flaring. A local tough guy named Marcos jutted his face into Waggy's, demanding revenge. He was a small man, but tough looking, and the mob was egging him on. They wanted blood, McClure's blood.

"Waggy, you see that, *mira eso*!?" the little tough guy said. "That *gringo* shit threw the contest to Gabby. He disrespected us! Gabby is one of us. He would have won without this bullshit. This is an insult! Somebody should fuck that guy up!" The mob roared its approval of Marcos. Things were getting out of hand. Director Vega watched the entire scene from the platform. Something had to be done. If Waggy could not contain the situation and it escalated into violence, it would end up on the news and spread throughout the surfing world. The integrity and professionalism of the *Asociación Profesional de Surfing de Puerto Rico* would be impugned, and the reputation of Rincón and Puerto Rico itself would suffer. Meanwhile, Waggy was hard at work trying to calm things down.

"Why did the *gringo* do this?" Waggy asked Marcos rhetorically, trying to engage him in dialogue.

"It's racism," Marcos responded. "Fuckin' racism."

"Well, maybe the judges will kick him out of the finals," Waggy said. "What the *gringo* did was very wrong, very disrespectful. We will discuss it with Contest Director Vega." Meanwhile, up on the platform Vega asked for two judges to go with Chief Judge Hector Guzmán down to the beach to interview McClure, support Waggy, and try to calm down the assembled mob.

"I'll go," said Cal Ritchie. "I know the players."

"Cal, *todo tranquilo*, okay?" Vega advised.

"Gotcha boss,"

"Iséla, *vete tu también*," Vega said to Judge Ruiz. "Don't say anything about the final results, just ask questions – go with Hector and back up Waggy." Judge Guzmán came to Vega with the contest rule book and drew the director off to one side.

"*Mira Jefe*," he counseled Vega. "Here it is, page 70 to 80. We can disqualify McClure for conduct that disrespects the Corona Circuit, the judges, the spectators, or his fellow competitors. Look at the people here, the spectators are insulted and disrespected by his actions. His behavior disqualifies him. He could have just ridden a shitty wave, or missed a wave and let the heat end. Plus, he used alcohol before the heat. It is forbidden. His conduct has caused damage to the image of surfing and the reputation of the *Asociación*. The record is clear. McClure is out, disqualified. Padilla moves up to second place. Everyone will be happy."

"Okay. *¡Eso es! Gracias,* Hector," Vega said. "*Baja allí con Cal y Iséla, hable con* Waggy, and then come back up here. Waggy can tell the people that we are taking care of it, and we will make a public announcement."

Gabby Cabrera was awarded first place in the men's division of the 2009 Corona Pro, Guillermo Padilla took second, and the young Brazilian Bino Medina placed third. In the women's division, Lila Lebrón won first, giving her enough points to re-enter the world tour competitive circuit, while Amory Murphy took second, and Roberta Lima third. Director Vega and Chief Judge Guzmán went up on the stage with Waggy Moreno standing close behind them. Video cameras streamed live, photographers and reporters from the surf media captured images for their news reports and interviews, but none of them except *The Inertia* mentioned the McClure affair, that he had thrown the contest and was disqualified, and that the crisis was now safely over with McClure as the scapegoat. Order had been restored in the order universe. Waggy persuaded everyone to chill out, and even Marcos gave McClure a friendly fist bump.

McClure later told me he didn't really give a shit, anyway. He didn't believe in surf contests. He wanted Gabby and his wife to have the prize money because they just had given birth to a baby boy and were dead broke. Over a beer at my house McClure showed me an excerpt from Plato's *Republic*, where Glaucon asks Socrates if there are good things in life, purely enjoyable things like surfing, harmless and fun, things you don't do for money or some other goal. You just do them because they are enjoyable for what they are in themselves (the *ding an sich* thing again), with no other motive. Surfing for the sake of surfing. Paddle out and smile. One and done. I felt I understood the wild 'wild card' Aidan McClure, a young man who knew enough to know himself. As Gerry Lopez once said, "All I really need is a rack of surfboards, a pair of trunks, some wax, and a car. The rest of the stuff is incidental."

McClure had realized Lukács' insight that economic relations are relations of people with people, not things with things. We are not economic 'things' on a vast spinning roulette wheel, although to some economists and business news editors that's pretty much all we are, essentially; individual beings compelled to fuck each other for money. But money does not buy freedom, because freedom is not for sale. You have to find it, earn it, live it. Aidan McClure had penetrated a fundamental truth.

NOTEBOOK 7

Deception don't preclude
a search for conviction.

Cy Tolliver, *Deadwood*

Notebook 7

Tuesday morning, 27 January
8:40 a.m.

Personae de Cork O'Reilly

With the contest over things settled back to normal in Rincón. The sky was gray. It rained, and then went totally blue, with little wispy clouds floating out to sea. The bars and guest rooms emptied out. The surf dropped down to a less scary mode of production, and the roads in and out of town drained the tourists, the vans, the campers, and the long lines of motorcycles. The *Paso Fino* equestrians galloped to their ranches in the hills and valleys, and the surfing pros skipped town for the next stop on the circuit.

Last night I went to Mikey's bar to see José and Dolores Muñiz, and Mary and Cork. Mikey Surf and Monica were sitting at a table in the back. Mary was really pissed at Cork, sitting by herself at the end of the bar. It was Cork's last night in Rincón and they were definitely splitting up. In true form, he berated me for my failures in the love category, as if I wasn't already deeply aware of them.

"What is it with you, man?" Cork said to me. "I bring an attractive woman to your house. She wants to fuck you, and you fall asleep during sex and pass her off to Mikey Surf! What the fuck, Brendan?"

"Dude, I'm just tryin' to find the right woman. It's not easy. And I didn't pass her off to Mikey, she *went to* Mikey. Women do that. So you need to ease up on me. It's not like you're a relationship counselor or something."

"Dude, I'm your best friend and you need sex counseling. If you're goin' gay on me we need to talk. You can't pull shit like that on me without talking first... we're brothers. You can't do that to a brother."

"I know that," I said. "Jesus, ease up Brah, you've got nothing to worry about. Take care of your relationships, and I'll take care of mine. How many girlfriends do you have now, anyway? Two or three? Four?"

"I don't know exactly, my brother. It might be two, two and a half; close to three. Mary's moving to Philly. Yvonne wants to come to New York with me. What the fuck am I supposed to do? I'm just tryin' to keep everybody happy."

"Cork, why don't you go sit with Mary. She looks pretty fucking lonely over there. You guys had a nice run. Be a gentleman and go over and talk to her. Tell her you love her and you're sorry you're so fucked up. It'll make her feel better."

"Okay, but Dude, I'm stopping by your house later to set those rabbits and birds free," Cork said. "I'm going to use the wire cutters from your shed in the back."

"This animal liberation gig is on you," I replied. "The people next door are my neighbors. I need plausible deniability."

"Like Nixon and Reagan?"

"*Exacto, mi amigo.*"

"So the Marxist goes Republican?"

"Flow with the river, Brah." Cork went down bar to sit with Mary. I slid over to sit with Dolores and José.

"That's some friend you have," Dolores observed.

"His life is one shitshow after another, but he's been like a brother to me. And now his girlfriend flirts with me. It's ridiculous."

"Mary likes you, man," José put in, "she's always liked you, Bro. I been seeing it all year. Look at them," José said, gesturing at Cork and Mary, who were bickering fiercely at the other end of the bar.

*

Mikey Surf was at a table in the back with Monica, captivated by her eyes and straw yellow hair.

"Do you want a ride to the airport tomorrow?" Mikey asked her.

"Sure."

"I was thinking I want to come up to New York in a couple of weeks to see you. I need to dry out; get healthy. I want to go to that Zen Center on 23rd Street. Are you cool with that?"

"Sure. You can stay with me. I'll go to the Zen place with you. I always wanted to check it out."

"Really, you will?"

"Sure." She gazed into Mikey's eyes and held them. She was so quietly sexy.

"Follow me, I'll show you my office and the back,' Mikey said. "Bring your drink." They walked to the door that led to Mikey's office and the back storeroom.

"Here's where I keep all the booze, et cetera," he said, opening the storeroom door.

"Oh really, do you fuck your girlfriends in here?"

"Only if they're nice to me – like you." Mikey took her body and pressed her flesh against his. He felt the curve in the small of her back, and her butt bumping out nicely. They kissed, and it was good, and they went into Mikey's office. He swept the papers off the desk and Monica sat on it. He helped her slip off her flimsy dress and underwear, and they made love with Mikey standing up going straight into her with his thick cock, as she reclined back, soft, freckly, wet.

*

Upon leaving the bar Cork drove with Mary to her house in the hills and around 1 a.m. he got up from bed, grabbed his keys, and prepared to depart, which upset Mary.

"You're going out to see Yvonne now on your last night here? What the fuck, Cork!"

"No baby, I'm definitely *not* going to see Yvonne. I wouldn't do that on our last night. But there's something I have to do. I'll be back in fifteen or twenty minutes, trust me."

"Trust *you*?"

"Baby, it's an animal liberation thing. I have to free the little rabbits and birds at Brendan's. It's true. Ask him tomorrow. I'll be right back."

Cork drove down the hill and parked out of sight two blocks up *Calle José Perez*. He walked down the street, snuck around the house to my garden shed in the back yard, got the large wire cutters, and went out the back gate onto the beach. The moon was high and full. The ocean's breast glittered in the moonlight. Cork walked south in the moist sand and then cut through Don Carlos' cow pasture to my next door neighbor's yard. Baby, the calico cat, confronted him in a small clearing. She rubbed his leg, looked up at him with her big eyes, meowed a few quiet words, and then watched him closely as he crept through the pasture to the cages under the neighbor's house. Upstairs a large flat screen blared a TV show in Spanish, extremely loud. They would not be able to hear him downstairs. He went first to the big white rabbit locked up with the black and orange rooster, cut the door off their cage and dropped it to the ground. Both animals jumped out to freedom and scattered into the cow pasture. Then he went to the row of rabbit cages on the floor and cut the doors off each one. The rabbits hopped away. Next he went to the plump black and white songbirds living on a mountain of their own shit and cut open the front door of their hell-world. They flew away into the night. He swept hens and chicks out of their cages as they clucked and squeaked, and then he ran through the pasture back to his car and drove up the hill to Mary's house.

*

The next morning Mary woke up in a cacophony of bird language; orioles, mourning doves, and black split-tail grackles. Cork lay alongside her, snoring.

She looked over at his Irish bulk, his stupidly handsome face and gently receding hairline. He was so innocent asleep, so guilty awake. He had cheated on her one too many times. The latest deception with Yvonne was enough. She would leave him to his mendacious games and fakeries. It was time to separate her karma from his. Philadelphia would be good. There would be interesting people on the Penn campus, and the fellowship at the medical school would be intense, but rewarding. Mary could see a future based on her own aspirations and ethics, not his bullshit. Yet, she reluctantly admitted to herself that she did appreciate Cork's bizarrely indefatigable spirit, his formidable belief in himself, and his cynical Irish New York wit.

He had developed a ridiculous self-narrative, in her view, but it was his own. It was original. No one had imposed it on him. He made it up himself, and it seemed to grant him a modicum of freedom. She had been willing to marry him and bear his children, but now it was over, like a death, a life that ended. He had taken too much. You cannot take too much.

A rumble emanated from Cork's belly and he coughed, turned over, and woke up facing her. She looked more beautiful than ever, a dream, his guardian angel.

"What's up honey?" he gargled.

"Nothing. You need to get back to Brendan's and pack for your flight this afternoon. We're done. It's you and Yvonne now, and whoever else you're fucking. You want her? Now you got her. I'm out."

"Oh Baby, I fucked up," Cork remonstrated. "I never should have gone to New York with her. I'm sorry Baby, can we just move on? You know I love you."

"No, I can't just move on. That doesn't work for me, Cork. You want everyone else to move on while you do whatever the fuck you want. I feel bad for Yvonne. She doesn't realize that being in love with you is the worst way to get close to you. The closer we come, the further you push us away. But she'll figure it out. Everybody does. Call a car and get out. I need you to get out." Mary was crying lightly. Cork turned over and buried his face in the pillow. Mary left the room.

"Mare, can you at least take me to the airport? Cork called out.

"No, sorry. Call Ramón or something. I'm really done."

*

Ramón picked up Cork a half-hour later. Like many Puerto Rican men of around eighty years of age, Ramón looked sixty-five. He was a taxi driver who knew everything that happened in the ex-pat world of Rincón. His family had been *Rinconeños* for generations, so he also knew everything that happened in the native community as well. He could remember when broad fields of sugar cane went right up to the beach and there were no houses, just cane blowing in the wind, and a narrow dirt path in and out. "If you wanted to eat, you hacked sugar cane," Ramón would say. "No work, no food; fifty-cents a day."

At eighteen Ramón moved to New York to live in Spanish Harlem. His first job was washing dishes, then a line cook, then he opened his own *colmado*, and then finally a restaurant and bar at 115th Street and Madison Avenue. He worked 7 days a week for twenty-eight years and retired to the *isla*. Now he drove people to the airport; drunks home from bars, and women home from their lovers' *bohios* in the hills of *Calvache*. He knew who sinned and who didn't, who was cheating, and who wasn't. He knew their children and their children's children. He knew who did cocaine and who refrained, and took them all to the airport and back again. High on coke and *Medalla* beer they told him everything, and he remembered it all. He would pick them up at the airport a year later and recite back everything they said; who they worked for, where they lived, their children's names, where they went to college, the health of their parents.

Ramón was well versed in Cork O'Reilly's manifold sins. He knew Dr. Mary North, and he had known Yvonne Acevedo since the day she was born to his second cousin thirty-one years ago. Ramón kept an ice chest full of cold beer in his taxi. He gave one to Cork and nudged him to tell him everything illegal and sinful that had transpired in the ex-pat world during the past few months. That was how you rolled with Ramón.

Cork checked in at the Jet Blue gate and walked down to the beach to kill time before his flight. He sat on a clump of weeds on a ridge overlooking the surf, watching sets of glassy 3 – 6 ft. waves roll in. His left leg was creased over his right thigh, with his back straight and upright. It felt good; the ocean's murmur, the dull thud of waves curling over the reef. After a few minutes he felt the ocean breathing through him and in him, and he thought, "my lungs are inhaling and exhaling, breathing with the whole ocean, and everyone and everything; the whole planet is breathing in and out with me, a cosmic egg in the ocean of being."

He sat very still. He wished Mary was with him so they could talk and make things right again. After twenty minutes he got up and walked back to the airport. Something had just happened. He wanted to savor it, and tell the Zen teachers in New York about it. Maybe that was what they called 'enlightenment.' He would go to the zendo on 23rd Street and find out.

Thursday a.m. 29 January

> For heaven on earth is a state of consciousness.
>
> Tom Blake, Surfing Pioneer

Martyrdom to Venus

I got up and made coffee. Cork and Rory were gone. I cleaned up the downstairs, gathered up the dirty sheets and towels and took them to the outside shower. I washed them by hand and hung them out to dry in the hot sun. Alan and Dobie, the north side neighbor's dogs, were running up the beach chasing a fat green iguana. The iguana was petrified, flapping its legs and five-fingered hands furiously on the sand to escape, but the dogs were gaining on him. Sensing doom, the iguana dove into the ocean and swam out five or ten yards. Alan and

Dobie plunged in but the lizard ducked below the surface, swam out another twenty yards, and disappeared. A few minutes passed and the iguana didn't surface, so Alan and Dobie swam back to the beach, forlornly staring out to sea, whining and barking. The iguana stuck its head up through the surface periodically to locate the dogs, and then dropped down into the water again. After five or six minutes Alan and Dobie gave up and went back to their house. The iguana watched them and swam back in unscathed, scurrying down the beach and ducking into Don Carlos' cow pasture for cover.

When I finished hanging the towels and sheets on the line, I grabbed my longboard off the back porch, brought it around front and flipped it onto the roof of the Explorer. My next door neighbor Rick Spinoza was watering plants and flowers in his front yard. He had brown color-treated hair streaked with thin lines of gray. A retired ironworker, Rick kept his front and back yards meticulously trimmed and sculpted. He watered the plants and trees daily, swept and hosed down the *marquesina*, and raked fallen palm leaves and branches. He was a compactly muscular man who spoke in the peculiar Philadelphia-inflected diction of South Jersey, the vowels contorted into warps that only Philadelphians and South Jerseyans could construe.

I was standing on the Explorer's sideboards tying down the rack straps over my surfboard while Rick raked grass and fallen palm leaves along the fence-line. He was a neighborhood philosopher who invariably brought up relevant and worthwhile topics to discuss, e.g., the functionalities of meditation, the nature of consciousness, the good life, etc. He stepped up to the fence to address me, rake in hand, and asked if I had meditated this morning. It went something like this.

"Hey Rick, yep, I did meditate... long enough to settle in and see the anger and how it's separate from me. My wife died. My friends are assholes. I need to move on, but it's tough."

"That's right, Brendan. You don't need the anger," Rick said. "Your friends are not helping you. When you meditate, shine the light in the front door and out the back door. Enlightenment is about waking up."

"I know Rick, but it's hard for me since Janice died. My friends don't know what I'm going through. They drink and carry on like teenagers and constantly push women on me. It's too much karma, Rick. I can't handle it."

"Brendan, when your friends are assholes, stop them! Stop their karma from leaking into yours," Rick declared, jabbing the rake in the air. "Your mistake is you have expectations of people. Don't expect anything from them." At that moment a pack of dogs went trotting out Rick's front gate, with Alan and Dobie in the lead. They marched up *Calle José Perez* in single file and cut into Don Carlos's field to hunt iguanas.

"My friends call me on the phone and say, Rick, hello, Rick! You've got to come over and help me take care of this shit I've created. We need you!" And I say to them, "No, I'm sorry, I can't do that. Only you can do that. Why should I waste my time trying to solve your problems? Only you can solve your problems!"

"Back in the day we believed in the Wizard of Oz," Rick continued, leaning over the fence. "The big guy in the sky was the president of everything, the magician. But we don't need him now, we know everything. You just have to want it, Brendan," Rick said decisively, and went back to his raking.

What Rick said made a lot of sense. It was remarkable how a regular working class Philly guy had such insight. How did he do it? Suddenly Rick stopped raking and looked straight at me, clutching the rake with two hands.

"Your job is to stay awake, Brendan," he said. "I get rid of my filters every morning when I wake up. Children lack filters, they have pure consciousness. Get rid of your filters, Brendan!" Then he shoved the rake right into my face, an inch from my nose.

"Is this one or two?"

"One," I blurted. Rick's face broke into a broad grin. He was immensely pleased. I had passed his *kōan*. I got in the truck and drove out *Calle José Perez* to surf up north, thinking that Rick must have studied Zen somewhere, maybe on a weekend retreat. Maybe he went to Tassajara Zen Mountain Center one summer, or maybe he had read up on Meher Baba. He must have read something. Had he studied Gurdjieff and hung out with the Gurdjieffians? They were pretty offbeat. It could definitely be them.

*

After a half-hour I turned off *Ruta Dos* onto a dirt road just past the airport that ran for two or three miles along a beach rimmed by jungles and abandoned fields, not far from where Cork had his enlightenment experience. Several surf spots were visible from the road, most of them empty or with just one or two surfers out. I drove to the end and pulled up to a line of trees at the water's edge to look at the waves. Mary North's Suburu wagon was parked a few cars down. She was on the north peak picking off glassy waves in the 3 – 6 ft. range, surfing with flair and confidence. On the narrow strip of beach below the parking area I recognized a guy I knew from Jersey, Vinnie Marsilio, with his cousin Nick, and a local guy named Maso. They were accompanied by a posse of young women in bikinis. Between drags on a thick joint Vinnie, Nick, and Maso were cutting two-by-fours and banging them into a rough wood staircase from the parking lot down to the beach. Vinnie was the type of guy who always made atrociously humorous comments. He would say the most ridiculous retro things on really serious topics of culture or politics, but coming out of his mouth they were hilarious and wryly brilliant.

Along the Jersey beaches where I grew up Vinnie Marsilio was considered a nut case. 'Normal' suburban people avoided him, but when those same suburbanites came to Puerto Rico to surf, all they wanted to do was hang out with Vinnie every day because of the Vinnie stories they could bring back home. He noticed me standing up on the ridge just above them looking out at the waves.

"Hey Binky, get down here and stop staring at that blonde chick Mary. Get over here and take a toke on this joint."

"I can't smoke and surf, Vinnie, it ruins my balance," I replied. "What are you guys doing, building stairs?"

"Yeah, stakin' out the territory for my little mafia here, Binko. You know Maso and my cousin Nicky, right? This is Darlene, that's Tracy Wong, and this is Yasmin. Darlene, could you give Professor Binky the joint? His name is Brendan, but I call him Binky 'cause he's uptight all the time. The guy needs to chillax."

"Where do you teach?" Darlene asked, as I took a hit on the joint.

"Oh, just U.P.R. Mayagüez; English lit., Caribbean lit."

"Binky, don't try anything," Vinnie interjected. "Darlene is a nice girl from Cali. She's in a university, like you. Tell him, Darlene."

"I'm in grad school at Berkeley, comp. lit."

"See Binky, not all my friends are stupid like Nicky and Maso. Darlene goes to Berkeley. Tracy here goes to U.S.C., and Yasmin goes to U.P.R. Mayagüez with you. Yazzy, do you ever see Binky on the campus in Mayagüez?"

"Yeah, I've seen him. But I never talked to him."

"Why not, Yaz? Why didn't you hit him up?" Yasmin made a funny face.

"Because he doesn't look at anyone. He walks around campus with his head down, looking at the ground, or something."

"Wow, Yazzy! What an observation. How come Nicky and Maso never say smart shit like that?"

"Because they're men, and men have cocks," Yasmin replied matter of factly, "and when you have a cock it's difficult to think, and it's difficult to notice what's going on around you." Everyone had a good belly laugh.

I watched Mary ride a few waves. She surfed smoothly, flawlessly, with a natural muscle intelligence that could read the hydrodynamics of a wave like the avionics on a Boeing 767. I got my board off the roof and paddled out. Mary spotted me and waved. We surfed together for an hour or two. She kept paddling over to me, smiling and flirting; flirting too much I thought. I was determined to keep it cool. Cork was my friend. I didn't want to be anywhere near the inside of their crumbling relationship. Up in the parking lot getting ready to go back home, Mary came over to me as I was strapping my board on the roof.

"Brendan, let's get some lunch over at *Jobos*, I'm leaving pretty soon. I'll tell you about my fellowship at Penn, and you can tell me about that article you're working on about that poet – what's his name again?"

"Philip Whalen."

"Yeah, Whalen, sounds like an interesting guy. I love poetry."

"I really don't have time, Mary. I need to get back and finish writing that paper, maybe later this week before you leave."

Mary shook her head "no," but didn't say anything. I turned around. She was standing close, practically touching me. Her bikini bottoms were hung low on her hip bones, which were perked out like two sides of a saddle a cowboy could climb into. I noticed her hard nipples, one pointing east, the other west, and I felt an urge for her, like I always had, but I knew if I let this moment pass I could drive away and face Cork, and also avoid the acute embarrassment of my own dysfunctional sexuality.

"Come on Brendan," Mary pouted. "*Jobos* is five minutes from here, we can get a fish taco at that place on the water and stop at Bernhard Vega's shop and check out his boards. It'll take a half-hour at most." I hesitated and looked into her eyes for a sign, some kind of sign.

"Okay Doc," I said, "follow me, what's a half-hour in the general scheme of things?"

*

We sat outside on the pleasant wooden deck of the fish taco place overlooking *Playa Jobos*. Two Coronas with lunch led to a grainy lemon margarita after lunch. When I went to the bathroom to pee Mary ordered two more margaritas from the waitress and ran out to her car. She took two light orange-brown 20 mg. Cialis out of a container in the glove box, slipped them into her mouth and chewed them into small particles, then ran back to the table and spit the crumbled fragments into my drink, stirring it with a thin plastic straw.

"You got us a drink, thanks Mare," I said, having missed the pharmaceutical processing. "Stirred not shaken, huh?"

"Yeah, I like them stirred up, mixes up the lemon, Cointreau, andmargarita mix. Makes the tequila taste better."

There was a small to medium longboard swell hitting *Playa Jobos*. From the restaurant deck we could see the entire stretch of beach, with its three main peaks. On the far right a wedgey wave slammed into *Jobos'* huge coral rock, while on the middle slopey peak longboard waves rolled over flat coral to the sandy beach. After about twenty minutes I began to notice Mary more closely. Her pink, orange, and green tropical skirt was way up her thighs, and her tank top was slipping down off her shoulders. My cock got hard and pushed up my shorts.

"Well, we better go," I said. "We can stop at Vega's shop and look at his boards."

"Okay yeah, do you want them to wrap the left-overs?"

"Sure, thanks." We walked out to the parking lot with Mary carrying the bag of left-over tacos to my truck. She stood just inches from me so that when I turned around to receive the tacos I would understand that she wanted to have sex, her physical closeness being the feminine signal. It was an unmistakable signal.

"Here's your taco."

"Here's *your* taco," I leaned in, kissed her on the lips, put my right hand around her cute backside, and slipped my fingers between her two halves of lovely ass. We kissed furiously.

"This is fucked up. Cork's my friend," I said.

"We broke up. He's with Yvonne, don't you remember? And I'm moving to Philly next week."

"But it's so soon, Mary. Shouldn't there be a period of like – like 'mourning' or something, a break?"

"Brendan, he's been having an affair with Yvonne for two or three months, probably more. I know you guys are close so I'm not going to say anything. Anyway, he's in New York. Yvonne will fly up in a few weeks to be with him. So look, sweet man, I'm coming to your house and I'm going to get us something we can cook for dinner later. We're friends. We're adults. I'll see you around five or six."

"Okay friend."

I got in my truck, drove back to Rincón, showered, shaved, put on cologne and my favorite "I want sex" beach shirt, and sat at my desk to work on the Whalen paper. Janice stared at me from a photo on the bookshelf. She was alive. Her eyes cut through me like a laser. It was that "revision of categories" thing again. I used to joke her that she was the cool Jew from Newark; never too impressed by anyone or anything, especially the rich or famous. Then I heard her voice, it was either inside or outside me, I couldn't tell –

"You need to move on, Baby," her voice said. "I can't come back. Nobody comes back. And you'll be here soon enough. Everyone will. People are reluctant to be born, reluctant to die. So have fun with Mary. She's not a bad person. I love you, Beavis."

*

Mary arrived at my house with fresh raw pork chops from a butchery owned by a local farmer, cut from the pig that morning. The sinews were visible, with thick ribs of fat and spots of blood. I marinated them in olive oil, garlic, onions, pinot grigio, salt, pepper, and basil; and chopped cherry tomatoes, onions, and spinach for a side of basil tortellini. Mary seemed happy to hang out with me. She told me she was attracted to my quiet, scholarly ways; that Cork was a mean Irish bulldog, and that I was a nice Irish Setter.

I could see where things were going so I made a firm plan. I would kiss her a little bit, keep it in check, and then send her home so I could buy time and save face with Cork. Unbeknownst to me, however, Mary had circulated forty milligrams of chopped Cialis into my vascular system, and the pharmaceutical molecules were sending strong "sex now" messages to my cock.

While the pork chops were marinating we went into the living room to have a glass of wine and talk. Mary took a seat on the couch. I sat across from her. Her skirt was pulled seven-eighths of the way up her thighs. I could make out red silk underwear. She had on black pumps and a loose white tank top. My cock was becoming difficult to manage with any type of controlled rationality.

"I can't wait to see your book, Brendan," Mary said. "When can you show me something?"

"Probably late February or early March. I've got to go back to the library in Berkeley and get all the images. Whalen did a lot of cool drawings in his journals, some in color, plus calligraphy and other stuff. Kerouac has an awesome painting of him in there, too."

"Wow, that's so cool, Brendan. I really like literature. I read a lot of poetry in high school and college. Med school just takes so much out of you there isn't much time left to do anything else."

"Keep a journal. That's a great way to start. Dr. Williams kept a journal. He was a pediatrician, and a great writer; great doc too. You've got to check out his work."

"Yeah you told me about him. I'm going to start reading him when I get to Philly."

"Yeah, it's some coincidence, but he went to Penn medical school, too. The poetry center there is named after him." I went back to the kitchen to stir the veggies into the tortellini. Mary got up and followed me in.

"How's the tortellini sauce coming?" she inquired. I felt her tank top brush against my arm and I turned around towards her. Her eyes were bright blue. The tiny blonde hairs above her lips made me want to have sex with her; and her long legs went on and on and on. The tank top didn't quite reach her waist, so her stomach flesh was open and flat all the way down.

"I'm going to let this sauce marinate in its juices," I said. "Let's go out on the deck." The moon was a sliver of crescent resting in the night sky like a shallow bowl. Above it a star shone dimly, and just beneath it another star shined brightly.

"Is that the north star, up there by the moon?" I asked her. Mary put her wine glass on the balustrade and looked up.

"I think that's Venus underneath. Maybe that's Mars above it. I'm pretty sure they're planets, not stars."

"Wow. How cool. Space is infinite." She took out her phone and turned on the Google Sky app.

"Look, yes, that's Venus underneath. Above it's either Neptune or Mars. They're too close to tell. But it's one or the other, see?" I looked at the phone and sure enough, Neptune and Mars were right alongside each other, so it was impossible to tell which was which with the naked eye. She stood so close to me I could smell her. Then I turned and put my right arm around her, just above the rise of her ass, in the small of her back, and pulled her in close. She looked into my eyes and put her mouth on mine and we kissed, tongues rolling and sucking. Mary was delicious. Her body fit mine like a socket and a plug. I stroked the nice little places between her butt cheeks, and we made love. This broke several rules, both spoken and unspoken, but we did it anyway, for in that moment of space/time where past was future and future past, Janice Hirschorn, a bodhisattva-being late of nirvana, gave her express permission to Dr. Mary North of this dimension, to break the love-spell cast over me, Brendan McGuinness. She ordained and decreed that I was free to make love again with a bodily-form human being, and I sat in a chair on the deck and pulled Mary on top of me and we fucked and fucked and fucked until the chair came apart in pieces and broke apart flat on the tiled deck, but we didn't stop there. We made love on the tiles, she under me, then me under her. And that was that.

Saturday January 31

Things are gathering up more and more beauty in
themselves, and I notice the beauty, and I see that
ugliness is just the debased side of things, and
it doesn't touch the beauty; not that much anyway...
coming back to Zen practice I see things I forgot about.

Cork O'Reilly's Journal
New York
Friday Jan. 30, 2009

CORK'S NEW YORK

Saturday morning Cork woke up in his apartment on Charles Street in the Village and grabbed a cab uptown for coffee with his agent, who wanted to talk to him about a Hollywood production company interested in adapting one of his novels for a feature film. Later that afternoon he had an appointment with Kōshin at the Zen center for a 'refresher' instruction on zendo etiquette and tidbits of advice on Zen meditation, since he had not been practicing Zen regularly for a long while. He also signed up as an official member of the *sangha* so he could have private spiritual meetings with Norman Fischer, the senior teacher, and take part in retreats and other events as a full member. I felt good about this because I knew that if he got into a sustainable Zen practice with Norman as his teacher, it would help him in his life, the way he lives, the things he does, and the trouble he brings on himself.

When he walked back downtown from the zendo just before 5:00 p.m. he purposely avoided Hogan's Pub and the drug and alcohol abuse he might be tempted by there, and instead stopped at the Kettle of Fish tavern on Christopher Street for a glass of wine. It was early, and quiet. Only a few patrons were perched on their bar stools. Cork knew the owner, Patrick Daly, a friendly Wisconsinite and huge Green Bay Packers fan. At the far end of the bar, in the window alcove on Sheridan Square,

Cork noticed an attractive woman, thirty-something-ish, slender, with dark wavy hair tied loosely back. Her face was vaguely Mediterranean; perhaps Jewish, Italian, or Latin. Their eyes met two or three times, so finishing up his second glass of wine Cork walked over to the alcove and introduced himself. She had a steely guard up, but bright dancing eyes and a smile to keep company with. Her name was Francesca Antonini. She lived somewhere in Manhattan. All she would say was "uptown," not that he cared, just making conversation. He found her strangely compelling, but a little off, and when she talked about visiting her parents on a wealthy strip of Jersey coastline he sensed familial tension. Maybe, he thought to himself, Francesca was the brilliant failure, the weird one. It went through his mind that they were good Italian parents who tried to help her, but she was irremediable.

"Cork is a different first name. I can't say I've ever met a 'Cork' before. Is it Irish or Scottish or something?"

"Irish. After the city my grandfather was from." He asked her what she did. In New York, when you ask people what they "do," you're asking what they do for work. At bottom, it's a socioeconomic question and a lead-in to further economic inquiry. Young New Yorkers want to know how much money you make; or how much you might have in the near future. In the old days when apartment rents were calculated in the hundreds, the question didn't matter much. Now it was seen as more or less vital.

"I teach yoga," she responded. "I teach people how to live in enlightenment." Her answer set Cork on edge, since he had just arrived in New York immediately after what he thought of as an enlightenment experience on the beach in Puerto Rico. Her response was uncanny, because the Zen teachers he had been exposed to were always vague or non-committal on the subject of enlightenment, yet she claimed it right away, unhesitatingly.

"Wow, that's pretty cool," Cork replied. "I'm into Eastern religion myself. I've been studying buddhism again lately, and Zen meditation."

"Sure. I've been there. I help people come out of their enlightenment experience so they know what to do next. People today are fools. They know nothing about the universe. When I became enlightened I vowed to teach and share my wisdom with the world. Bliss, pure bliss." Wow, Cork thought to himself, this is really weird. This is someone who missed the train leaving the station. He decided to confront her.

"I'm not interested in bliss," Cork said. "I'm only interested in what's real. I'm a writer, so I'm aware that anyone can make things up." She pointed a finger to her heart. "It's all here, whatever I say."

"Whatever you say? So you teach? You have, like, a yoga center or a place where you teach?"

"Oh no, I contract with people; clients on the upper east side, upper west side. I can't just give to anyone – it's important to give – but if people can't receive, well it's just unproductive."

"Interesting," said Cork. "I have a teacher, have you ever heard of him, Norman Fischer? He's a Zen teacher, up on 23rd Street."

"No, I never heard of him, but I don't teach like that. It's right here," she said, snapping her fingers in the air over her head, "right in this instant moment. If you don't get it, it's a waste of time to talk to you – what's your name again?"

"Cork. Nice meeting you. You're Francesca, right?"

"Right."

Francesca Antonini claimed to be extraordinarily enlightened and told Cork flat out that he fell far short of her standards. She also said there was not much reason for them to talk again unless he wanted to study with her. In Cork's view the conversation verged on the grotesque. Cork had studied with some credible, certified buddhist teachers, and he had just come downtown from the zendo on 23rd Street. None of the teachers there, or anywhere, ever made extravagant claims about their own enlightenment. It was unprecedented, as far as he could tell. Still, it was at least interesting. Francesca departed the Kettle of Fish and when she was safely out the door the youngish bartender, in a skullcap and closely trimmed beard, leaned over and confided to Cork that Francesca was a nut job. Thank God for New York, Cork thought to himself, for keeping everything interesting and everyone on their toes.

20 February 2012

> Enlightenment enrages: for the slave wants the unconditional,
> he understands only what is tyrannical [...]
>
> Wherever on earth the religious neurosis has appeared
> we find it tied to three dangerous dietary demands:
> solitude, fasting, and sexual abstinence.

Friedrich Nietzsche, Das Religiöse Wesen

CORK'S TALK

Cork emailed me that he was invited to give the 'Beginner's Mind Talk' tomorrow morning at the Zen center on 23rd Street, a tradition at American Zen centers wherein a new student presents a discursive introduction to the community at large about how and why he/she came to practice Zen.

Rachel Rosenthal came in from Brooklyn for Cork's talk. Hank didn't come, but Mikey Surf came with Monica, as they now lived at Monica's place on the east side of Manhattan. The teacher Norman Fischer came this particular morning, too. Norman blends Zen Buddhism with his own unique brand of reform Judaism. He's a Zen Rabbi, so to speak, a priest and teacher who's carved out a highly idiosyncratic historico-religious path, blending Jewish culture, values, and rabbinical style with traditional Zen Buddhism. Truthfully, Judaism and Zen Buddhism share some religious practices and formations and certain vague facets of religious consciousness, having crossed paths in the Middle East and South Asia eons ago. Each side had, undoubtedly, taken something from the other.

Yet, some orthodox Jewish rabbis in New York and New Jersey despised Fischer because they intentionally misunderstood him. Their religious philosophy is very cool, very deep, and steeped in rich Jewish mystical traditions, but it allows for no (or very little) new information, and no new or alternative modes of spiritual practices of any type, at any level. They have a tight philosophical and religious lid on their thing. It works for them, so they have no desire for discovery, change, or evolution. The lid never ever comes off. They treated Norman like they treated Jesus of Nazareth; an outlier, a nut, someone to be shunned.

*

It was 10 a.m. and time for Cork's talk. He was raised Roman Catholic, not Jewish, so there was no reason for any inter-religious controversy. I watched the video of the talk that the Zen center posted on the Web. After bowing and offering incense, Cork ascended the Dharma Seat. Sitting upon the thick black cushion and crossing his legs Zen-style, he looked about the room and spotted Monica sitting next to Mikey Surf. Mikey proffered him a rather sour frown, but Rachel Rosenthal smiled at him from her seat far in the back. After a brief formulaic chant Cork began his talk.

"Good morning everyone. Thank you for coming. I want to thank our priests here at this temple, Kōshin and Chodo, both have helped me so much. I also want to thank my teacher Norman Fischer and everyone in the *sangha* for encouraging me to give this talk. Norman has been so good to me, so understanding of my faults and failings. It is encouraging to have a teacher who is so non-judgmental.

This is the first time I've had to talk publicly about buddhism. I am coming back to this practice after several years' absence, so there may be some rough patches. Although I more or less stopped practicing formally during the past few years, I started meditating and studying Zen again this past winter with my good friend Brendan McGuinness. We sat *zazen* at his house in Puerto Rico a bit, and when I was returning to New York he advised me to come here, connect with Norman, and try to get a better spiritual life going. Brendan's a good person, maybe some of you know him. He used to study Zen here. I took his advice because I wanted to change some things about myself, or at least explore them better. So here I am.

"I have been a writer of novels these past 15 years, not a very good writer, but a writer nonetheless, so my talk will not be too churchy. My books are usually about stupid selfish people; people who talk too much, drink too much, and run around the world in a state of hysteria and delusion. Sounds familiar, huh? I've never been married, so I bounced around. I felt like I could have married, I've been with some very nice people, but I always break it off after a year or so – I think my record is three years. . . I'm not exactly sure why. Maybe it's the drinking, maybe it's my wandering eye. The women I've been with are great, though, every one of them a saint. They'd have to be a saint to be with me. Sometimes I think that if Norman can help me with advice or guidance or something I will mend my ways, reform, and start to act like a normal person. I dunno. It's possible, right?" (Quiet guffaws and a trickle of laughter around the room.) Norman doesn't seem to judge much, but he did once say to me, "What are you missing because of the choices you've made?"

"That was a very good question. I've thought about it, and now I think I know what I've been missing. I've been missing almost everything for a very long time."

Cork scanned the room of devoted buddhists and random New Yorkers. Mikey Surf's face broke into a broad grin, and he spotted Rachel's calmly intelligent face in the back. She was sitting on a cushion on the bamboo *tatami* mats. They acknowledged each other.

"I have to say I was a crazy kid. I didn't respect my parents at all. And now, being older and wiser, I realize how good they were to me. They were a little bit bad, too, but nowhere as bad as I held them accountable for. They tried hard to be good – very hard, but they ended up both of them severe alcoholics. Plus my mother was bipolar. They didn't have a diagnosis for it back then, or any effective therapeutics, just a big scary mental hospital way out of town in the woods. We had a really crazy household. I didn't know of a single other family in our parish that was as insane as ours, except maybe the Donnelly's, down by the beach. The Donnelly's parents were demonstrably crazy. They had seventeen kids. Yes, seventeen. Of course that's what drove them crazy, but their religion was the root cause. They were unwaveringly loyal to the One Holy Roman Catholic Apostolic Church, the universal Church, the original thing itself, straight from Jesus. Catholics were required to have kids non-stop, without birth control – under pain of excommunication from the Church – which was equivalent to being sentenced to hell for all eternity. You definitely didn't want to be excommunicated from the One Holy Roman Catholic Apostolic Church. There was no redress, no cure.

"Mothers died because of this rule enforced by the male theologians in Rome. Families were devastated. Birth control was forbidden because of the weird philosophy that sex for sex's sake was evil. Sex was only okay for human reproduction. It was a job. And the job was to manufacture as many Catholic babies as possible, for heaven *and* earth. So it was political, although they never admitted it.

"Jesus' mother Mary was a virgin. Therefore Jesus wasn't conceived by sexual intercourse, he came directly from the Father in heaven, immaculately, without heterosexual sex. It's kind of a gay mythological construct, in my view. Not that there's anything particularly wrong with gay mythology, but what resulted was that the Church wouldn't let priests marry women or have girlfriends, so the only alternative was boyfriends and altar boys. But the Jews had it right again. They decided that pleasurable sex between parents was good thing for the marriage relationship, and therefore good for the whole family unit. That was smart.

"My friend Jackie was like the first or second oldest Donnelly boy. I can't remember which, there were so many of them. He was amazing on the lead guitar, a brilliantly wacko kid. We thought he was going to be the next Jimi Hendrix, but there was only one problem. Jackie never left the house except to go to school. They lived in a huge Victorian pile two blocks from the beach and he would sequester himself all weekend in a distant room on the third floor to practice guitar riffs on his Fender Stratocaster. In the entire universe of New Jersey only me and Neil Hickey, who lived down the street from the Donnelly's, knew what a great guitar player Jackie was. The problem is if you never leave the house to play gigs or do jam sessions with your friends and fellow musicians, no one gets to see your talent.

"Bruce Springsteen, who lived nearby, was lucky. His parents abandoned him and moved to California, so he didn't have pain-in-the-ass parents at home anymore. In the wild 1960s and 70s that was the best thing that could happen to a rock n' roll musician. You could do whatever the fuck you wanted with whomever the fuck you wanted to do it with. Bruce went out into the world with his guitar and lyrics and played gigs all over the Jersey Shore. But Jackie's parents never left home. It squashed his music career. Imagine Jimi Hendrix playing up in that room on the third floor. He'd still be alive today.

"Anyway, I think I finally understand the Buddha's teaching that life is suffering and human existence is basically unsatisfactory. I know this because everything hurts now. Everything I do. Everything I did. Everything I didn't do. It hurts. I feel it, and I don't know what to do about it. Norman says "just sit with it. Try to sit still with it, watch it, take care of it." Seems like pretty good advice.

"The other thing is, being raised Roman Catholic and going to Catholic school, there were nuns and priests everywhere. We had religion class every day with Sister Alma, a sweet and pious woman, political science class with Sister Vincent, a flaming leftist, and we had the ritual of mass every Sunday. Our parish was a lot like American Zen Buddhism today, with the black robes and the dour priests. We had incense, statues, iconography, symbols, texts, and commentaries all the time. Also, everyone we knew was Catholic. I met a Protestant kid once in eighth grade and I asked him, how could you leave the Church like that and cut it in half?

"The Jews we understood. Jesus was originally Jewish. It was the Protestants we couldn't figure out. Zen Buddhism is a bit like Catholicism to me. In Catholicism we had Holy Communion. It made you feel better, plus your sins were forgiven and you felt a little holy. In Zen Buddhism you have *zazen* and *dokusan,*[12] and they make you feel better, and you feel a little holy. Plus you have male and female priests, and they don't care if you're gay. That's one difference right there. Maybe Catholics should do that, you know, join the 21st century.

"My only issue right now with Zen Buddhism is that I can't figure out what 'enlightenment' is. Maybe it's just to live a good life and be non-dualistic in your thinking, in your approach to life. It makes sense. It made sense to Jack Kerouac. He was a writer and a lifelong Catholic who became a Buddhist, at least for a while. I think he tried to combine both religions in his head syncretically, but left them sitting there like an apple and a pear. Maybe he did this so he could be true to his mother. She was heavily Catholic like my mother, and she didn't want him to abandon Jesus, Mary, and the saints. Kerouac wanted his mother to be happy, so he went back to Roman Catholicism at the end of his alcoholic life just to make his mom happy. I can see me doing that for my mother too, eventually. When she was alive I couldn't do it because I thought she was too crazy. Plus, I concluded that Roman Catholicism was vastly inferior to Zen Buddhism. Now I'm not so sure.

"What the fuck, right? Who cares? I really never knew anything, anyway. Sorry, by the way, for the expletive. I hope no one was offended. I'll end now with my big *kōan* question. Can a person be crazy and still be enlightened? Could you be neurotic, a drunkard, or just fucked up? Or does the buddhist enlightenment preclude craziness of all kinds? If your answer is "yes" then I think you might be the fox in the Fox *Kōan.* Thank you very much for listening."

Cork's Beginner's Mind Talk was over, and the assembly did the chants and bows that follow a talk or sermon in the zendo. He found Rachel Rosenthal waiting for him in the lobby.

"How was it Rachel, was it okay? I was a little nervous."

"Yes, you were fine," Cork. "I thought the Kerouac stuff was really interesting. Do you really think that much about Catholicism and Buddhism?"

---

[12] A private spiritual meeting with a priest or religious teacher, not entirely dissimilar from the formal Roman Catholic confessional.

"Yeah, sometimes."

"I thought you were great, honestly," Rachel said. "People like a little wild crazy as long as you don't go into too much detail. What are you doing now? Do you want to have a drink with me somewhere?"

"I'd love to, Rachel, can we rain-check it? I've got to meet a friend. But I'd love to hang out with you. Let's do something next week. I'll text you." Rachel leaned up and kissed Cork on the cheek, in a friendly way. But Cork could tell she liked him. There was something about her. Maybe salvation. They parted and Cork hailed a cab to the Kettle of Fish pub in Sheridan Square.

Sunday, February 22
9:39 a.m.

Barrio Ensenada, Rincón

Cork emailed me about his talk at the zendo. He thinks he has a crush on Rachel. He thinks she might be the only person in the world who could kick his ass and straighten out his emotional life. But I don't think she'll leave Hank. Their kids are too young, plus Jews don't do that kind of a thing, not that often anyway.

He also told me about 'enlightened' Francesca at the Kettle of Fish. I fail to understand why he spends so much time cultivating crazy people. About her, all I can say is there's no end to the possibilities of the human imagination. And I thank the gods for serious philosophers like Norman, Janice, Fredric Jameson, and Nietzsche.

*

Mary has departed for Philly and Penn. There must have been a lot of pent-up erotic energy floating in the atmosphere between us because we had outrageously good sex before she left. I like her, but I don't think I'm in love. She's smart, fun, attractive, and a good surfer, but for me it's just too close to her relationship with Cork. Anyhow, how would we conduct a relationship with her in Philly and me in Rincón? She'll be completely tied up in her medical studies at Penn, with little or no time to visit me in Puerto Rico.

I took a beach walk this morning and ran into Rick Spinoza again. He was tossing a ball for Alan and Dobie in the tide pools. There is something extraordinarily human about Alan. He is a mid-size dog with brown, white, and black hair, and the facial expressions of a human being, so he is extraordinary to be around, and he is clearly delighted to be around people. Everyone notices it. It makes one wonder about the being-in-the-world consciousness of our mammalian cousins. We have so much in common with them physiologically, but we know so little about their interior consciousness, their psychology. What is their thinking like? Is it all imagistic, like hieroglyphs? Could there be human-language words lodged within their cognitive mental structures? Our dog Coquito knew at least a hundred words. What about syntax? How do they put it together?

Walking on the beach with Rick he advised me to move in with Mary in Philadelphia and get a teaching gig up there somewhere. But I couldn't fathom missing the winter season in Rincón. Maybe next year, I told him, or the year after.

END

ACKNOWLEDGMENTS

I would like to acknowledge the kind assistance of the
following people who aided me immeasurably through the
various personal, editorial, and creative processes necessary
for the completion of this book.

Valerie Krishna
Claire Talbot
Richard Sieburth
Sara Snow
Carl Nagin
Tom Ingalls
Jordan Thorn
Arnie Kotler
Arlene Lueck
Ashley Lloyd Thompson
Ward & Paula Smith
Frosty Hesson
Howard "Boots" McGhee
Ray & Lisa Licata
Mario Kinkela
Dermot McEvoy
Norman Fischer
Brian Finn
Megan Lotter
Jimmy Bonet

Steve Fitzpatrick
Greg Carson
Phil Painter
Steve Wyeth
Werner Vega
Michelle Diaz
Valerie Evans
Alberto Padilla
Leon Richter
Alex Thompson
Tim Brennan
Robin "Zeuf" Hesson
Carmelita McGhee
Coral Baugh
Luly Soto
Dennis Ritch
Fiore De Castro
Lenny Intreglia
George Ruggles
Migdalia Bonet

THE TEXT

This book was compiled from hand-written
journal notebooks, except for much of the later
material, from 2009 to 2012, which derives from
journal entries recorded in several laptops.

ILLUSTRATIONS

COLOPHON

TYPOGRAPHY

Chapparal Pro, Seriffa, Attic

PAPER

PRINTING & BINDING

McNaughton & Gunn, Saline, Michigan

DESIGN

Ingalls Design, San Francisco
Tom Ingalls and Megan Lotter

MISSING
LINKS
PRESS